Eyes firmly on the ball a determined Alan Smith of Arsenal tries to shoot for goal before Forest's Stuart Pearce gets a chance to stop him.

© IPC MAGAZINES LTD 1989

# LIVE

## Gunners wrecked our double dream

**T**he look of dejection on my face after Arsenal had snatched the League Championship from our grasp in the last seconds of the season told the whole sad story. I was totally drained, physically and mentally.

We had wanted to win the title for the 95 who died at Hillsborough and to have been denied what would have been a remarkable League and FA Cup double was a bitter pill to swallow.

But full credit to Arsenal for the way they stuck to their own task. Few people would have given them much of

*Michael Thomas scores Arsenal's winner that gives them the Championship and broke my heart.*

# R - CRUEL

hope of beating us by two clear goals at Anfield on the last day of the season would they?

Perhaps the effects of a long, demanding season had taken their toll. We will never know.

Under the circumstances though, finishing second to Arsenal and winning the FA Cup wasn't such a bad achievement and we should be proud to have come so close to the double.

All in all it was a season which, for very different reasons, will stay in the memory for a long time. Here are some of the dates to remember …

### August 20, 1988
### Liverpool 2 Wimbledon 1
After losing out to Wimbledon a few months before in the FA Cup Final we were doubly determined to put the records straight when we met again in the Charity Shield. I know which trophy I would sooner have won but I don't mind admitting that revenge was still sweet. It was certainly a special day for John Aldridge who, with Ian Rush back at Anfield and waiting in the wings, was under pressure to produce the goods. He did just that by scoring both goals. The Aldo one-two you might say.

### January 1, 1989
### Manchester United 3, Liverpool 1
You might think it strange that I should select a game which we lost so convincingly but the truth is that this defeat proved to be the turning point in our season. We had never really found our best form and this game at Old Trafford gave us the kick up the backside we really needed. We didn't lose again in League or Cup until the last game of the season. For the record I scored the opening goal before United hit back.

### April 15, 1989
### Liverpool v Nottingham Forest
The day of the illfated FA Cup semi-final at Hillsborough and the tragic loss of 95 lives. The disaster affected me deeply and had a profound effect on my attitude towards people that we so often take for granted. It can only be hoped that lessons have been learned from such a tragic occasion.

### May 7, 1989
### Liverpool 3, Nottingham Forest 1
A re-run of the FA Cup Semi-Final and an emotional occasion for all concerned. John Aldridge got two more vital goals and a Brian Laws own goal put the result beyond doubt.

### May 20, 1989
### Everton 2, Liverpool 3
The FA Cup Final and fittingly, on such an emotion-charged occasion, an all-Merseyside affair. The game itself was as dramatic as anything I've played in and you couldn't have written a script to do it justice. John Aldridge was on the mark (again!) and his fourth minute effort looked like winning the Cup until Stuart McCall struck an equaliser in the dying seconds. Enter Ian Rush. He scored twice in extra-time.

### May 26, 1989
### Liverpool 0, Arsenal 2
The most remarkable finish to a League season there has probably ever been. Unfortunately Arsenal were the ones who were celebrating after Michael Thomas had scored the all-important second goal in the dying seconds. I must admit I thought we had won the title, and the double, but Thomas showed what an unpredictable game football is.

# I'd ha
# George

# ve joined for £50 !

George Graham

**B**rian Marwood needed only 90 seconds to decide to take his special brand of wing play to Arsenal.

In fact Gunners boss George Graham would have got one of the bargains of the century if he could have discovered Marwood's mood while discussing the deal.

"He could have offered me £50 a week and I still would have signed," insists the former Hull City and Sheffield Wednesday winger.

"I had four happy years at Sheffield Wednesday, but the club's training methods eventually got to me. I think I became burnt out and it reached the stage where I would wake up in the morning and dread the thought of running up another hill.

"Arsenal, in comparison, are a very traditional club known throughout the world. There is an aura about Highbury and everyone from George Graham to the players feel very proud to be part of the club.

"I knew they were a good young side, so I thought I would be joining them at the right time."

So Marwood put pen to paper on a £600,000 transfer from Wednesday to Arsenal in March 1988.

And his success story began to take shape almost straight away. His first goal for the club came against Coventry from the penalty spot in Arsenal's penultimate game of the 1987-88 season.

He recalls: "The team had missed a few penalties before I arrived at the club, and I could see quite a few fans in the North Bank with their arms in the air waiting to catch the ball.

## Nice way

"Thankfully I managed to put it in the back of the net and it was a nice way to introduce myself to the fans."

To everyone at Highbury he suddenly became 'Brian Marwood on the wiiiiiing!' And, after only 15 League appearances for Arsenal (six goals) he made his England debut in Saudi Arabia at the age of 28.

He came on as substitute for just nine minutes and says: "If I never play for my country again at least I can say I wore an England shirt – and that means an awful lot to me."

Meanwhile, Arsenal's mightiest challenge for the First Division title in 18 years made Marwood's first season in the South a memorable one.

But don't ever call him an overnight success.

He says: "I got agitated when I realised that many people thought I had appeared from nowhere last season.

"I wasn't even playing the best football of my career – my form was just as good about four or five years ago at Sheffield Wednesday.

"The difference is that Arsenal get far more media attention than Wednesday. During my first couple of seasons in Yorkshire, in fact, Wednesday were doing better than Arsenal.

## Derogatory

"Unfortunately our achievements weren't enough for the football purists. We felt we didn't get the publicity our results deserved and it seemed the only time we were mentioned was in some sort of derogatory manner."

It would be true to say, however, that the lad brought up in a coal mining village near Sunderland has had to work hard to get where he is.

At his first club Hull, for example, he wondered whether he had a job at all when the club were threatened with liquidation.

Now though, midway through his three year contract with Arsenal, he can afford to look ahead with optimism.

"I'd love to stay at Arsenal beyond the end of my contract," he says. "And if a coaching job at Highbury ever came along that would be great." (Don't forget the fifty quid a week attitude, George!).

"If not then I'd think seriously about playing abroad before finishing my career or, even better, joining my home-town club Sunderland."

For £50 a week? We couldn't get an answer to that one.

Brian made his England debut against Saudi Arabia . . . alongside club-mate Tony Adams.

# ALEX
# CAP
## Dons' star

**R**ock star Rod Stewart didn't have to be asked twice to join the chorus of acclaim for Aberdeen and Scotland star Alex McLeish.

The pop veteran wasn't content just to sing the praises of the red-haired defender – he jumped at the chance to turn out in a Testimonial game that packed Pittodrie.

A full house of 23,000 saw Rod line up alongside his hero, Kenny Dalglish, for an international select that also included rival Old Firm skippers Roy Aitken and Terry Butcher.

McLeish, meanwhile, was in direct opposition as he teamed up again with the players who won the European Cup Winners' Cup when they defeated Spanish giants Real Madrid in Gothenburg in 1983.

### Hungry for success

That was just one of many prizes collected by The Dons during the reign of manager Alex Ferguson – and McLeish is hungrier than most for more success.

When Aberdeen failed to capture a major honour during the 1988-89 campaign it left a three-year gap since their last trophy success.

"That's too long for a club of our stature," moans the wholehearted defender. "Now that we've gone three years without winning a thing I appreciate our past success all the more.

"I suppose we were all a bit spoiled during those years when we won at least one of the major competitions every season.

"But don't think our glory days are all in the past. I'm confident about the future, so confident I really believe we're on the verge of doing something big all over again."

Players have come and gone since

# AIMS TO 'EM ALL!

## eyes his third World Cup Finals

named him as captain for the crucial World Cup qualifying game against France when a Mo Johnston double ensured a magnificent 2-0 home success.

It was in March, 1980, that McLeish celebrated his Scotland call-up with a starring role in the comfortable 4-1 Hampden triumph over Portugal.

Now, almost ten years on, he is fourth in the list of his country's most-capped players and aiming for his third appearance In the World Cup Finals.

Spain 1982, Mexico 1986 ... now his target is Italy and the 1990 final stages of the world's top competition.

McLeish first arrived at Pittodrie straight from school in his native Glasgow but he has no regrets at staying put.

His partnership with skipper Willie Miller, five years older at 35, is still the solid foundation it was when they first teamed up at the heart of The Dons' defence more than 500 games ago.

The double act has also served Scotland well. Apart from playing together in more than 40 senior internationals, both have gained the added distinction of captaining their country.

Both players have also gained their places in the Hampden Hall of Fame, an exclusive club for players who win 50 or more Scottish caps.

McLeish took his cap count to 60 when Scots boss Andy Roxburgh

**1** Talking about a possible meeting with Ruud Gullit in a pre-season tournament at Wembley featuring both Spurs and AC Milan he said: "I am looking forward to seeing him in action. I bet he's thinking the same about me."

**2** Outlining his ambitions after joining Spurs for £2 million he said: "In time I want to be recognised as one of the best players to come out of England, talked about in the same vein as Bryan Robson and Kevin Keegan."

**3** On the subject of a chocolate-free diet he claimed to be on, he said: "I haven't touched any sweets for months and I've become something of a salad freak so they can't call me the Mars Bar Boy any more. The Cucumber Kid is more appropriate now!"

**4** About his much-publicised return to Newcastle early in the season he said: "I dare say that some of the jokers in the crowd will throw Mars Bars at me, but I won't eat them. I'm off chocolate remember. I shouldn't mind some salad stuff though."

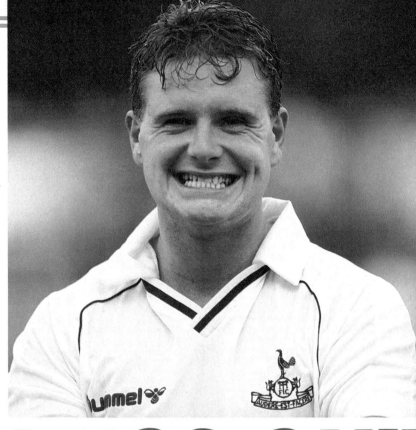

# 20 THINGS ONLY

## COULD

*A light-hearted look-back at the SHOOT star's first season as a* **Tottenham player**

**SNAPPY BIGSHOTS ...** *Gazza and team-mate Chris Waddle see the game from a different angle.*

**5** As people queued up to take a pop at him in the Press, Gazza declared: "John Bailey (my favourite cartoon character) was one of the first to go to the Press with stories of training ground bust-ups. I don't mind him selling his soul though, he obviously needs the money."

**6** After scoring against Arsenal with his boot off he said: "I suppose you could say I socked it to 'em."

**7** On the subject of star status he said: "I used to stand next to the likes of Rush, Robson and Dalglish and wonder what I was doing on the same field. Now I'm there alongside them as a top player in my own right ... and loving every minute of it."

Our star-writers Gazza and Tony Cottee brighten up the scene in Albania.

# GAZZA HAVE SAID

**8** Before his return match with 'nutcracker' Vinny Jones, he said: "We certainly don't hate each other as some people would like to think. In fact we are quite close – although not as close as we were at Plough Lane that time. Ouch!"

**9** About facing former Newcastle team-mate David McCreery, the man he describes as the 'best midfield marker in the country' he said: "The only way I'll get away from him is if I tie his boot laces together at half-time."

**10** After getting Fat Boy taunts from Millwall fans he recalled: "I stuffed the ball up my shirt and laid on the floor as if I was too fat to get up. I think they enjoyed it."

**11** On the subject of Spurs' return to form he said: "Things are going so well that even Terry Fenwick smiled the other day. He's from Sunderland, you see."

**12** His former Newcastle chairman Stan Seymour called Gazza 'George Best without brains' prompting this reply from our hero: "If he had said I was as handsome as George Best I wouldn't have minded."

**13** About criticism from the St. James' Park boardroom he said: "If the Newcastle directors continue to slag me off I will retaliate and I have got a suitcase full of stories which will expose and embarrass them."

**14** Of his effervescent nature he said: "At the end of the day it is all about confidence and you could say I was blessed with more than my fair share."

**15** After hitting a brilliant solo goal for England against Albania he said: "To score my first goal for England was unbelieveable. I have dreamed about that moment since I was knee high to a Mars Bar."

**16** Following even more criticism, this time by Sheffield Wednesday's Darren Wood who said he was too slow and wasn't world class, Gazza said: "I am now working hard to become as skilful and quick as him."

**17** Asked how he would describe himself in a Lonely Hearts column he said: "Good looking, boring, manic depressive, hates talking, dislikes sport and has no friends."

**18** Talking about people who made him laugh he said: "My Spurs team-mate John Moncur has me in stitches with his antics. He's even funnier than me ... well almost."

**19** On the subject of Chris Waddle's haircut he said: "He looks like he's been dragged through a hedge backwards ... twice."

**20** Asked if he would consider changing his 'daft as a brush' image Gazza said: "Never. If people don't like me as I am, tough." And so say all of us...

Lee Sharpe has made more progress than most young players, yet it was only a couple of seasons ago that he was told he was not good enough to make the grade in the Football League.

Wolves, Birmingham City and West Bromwich Albion all had opportunities to sign Lee, but in each case they did not rate him.

But Manchester United's Alex Ferguson is delighted with Lee Sharpe's form.

The 18-year-old has already been used in an assortment of positions at Old Trafford, proving his versatility and outstanding potential.

Fans watching him in the big matches at Old Trafford might be lost to understand how he was rejected not so long ago.

Sharpe said: "Kevin Reeves of Birmingham City told me I hadn't the enthusiasm, the dedication or talent to become a professional footballer.

"West Bromwich effectively told me the same thing when they said I should snap Torquay's hand off if they were prepared to offer me a YTS contract.

"At the time I thought it was their way of saying that was the best I could ever expect from soccer."

The young Midlander from Halesowen, however, took full advantage of the opening at Torquay and immediately made an impact on the West Coast.

# SHARPE almost quit

## 'Told I wasn't good enough', says young Man. United star

But one of the strange quirks of soccer is that he might even now not have been in the Football League.

Sharpe explains: "I joined them on the day after they had survived a Fourth Division play-off game. If they had lost and gone out of the Football League I would not be where I am today."

As a result Manchester United stepped in and paid a record £50,000 for the 16-year-old while other clubs, like Nottingham Forest, who have picked up several good players from the Birmingham and West Midlands area in recent years, hesitated.

Sharpe said: "No one can really appreciate just how close I was to quitting soccer at the time I joined Torquay. I was on £28 a week and it was only the support of my parents which kept me going.

"Now I am playing with some of the best players in the game and joining United is as high as you can go."

Despite all his success with United Sharpe is brought down to earth every training day because he still has to change with reserves.

He said: "The top players like Bryan Robson and company have their own room and I understand that you have to be a certain age before you are elevated to this position.

"I'm not complaining. I am enjoying everything at the present moment.

"One of my big ambitions is to play in an FA Cup Final at Wembley. Another is to play for the full England team."

Not bad targets for a youngster who was informed he wasn't good enough and later told that he would have to spend 12 months playing in Manchester United's reserves before he would be considered good enough for the first team.

# NIGEL CLOUGH
## Nottingham Forest

Teamwork may have been the secret of Norwich City's sparkling form last season – but the slimline tonic provided by winger Dale Gordon was undoubtedly a key ingredient.

The Carrow Road favourite shed a stone in weight during the summer of 1988 as he pounded the streets near his home in the seaside town of Caister and stuck rigidly to a diet supervised by girlfriend Lisa, now his wife.

"When I reported back for pre-season training I couldn't believe the difference," says the 22-year-old local boy made good.

"Being lighter made me feel better and I felt as if I could run all day. I was relaxed, confident and eager to get going – exactly the opposite to how I'd felt just a few months earlier.

"The previous season had been something of a nightmare for me. I wasn't playing regularly in the first team, then I dislocated my shoulder and never recovered in time to get back into contention.

"To be honest, I even thought of leaving Norwich. I'd seen other players come and go and I began to wonder if I'd be better off elsewhere."

Gordon, a member of The Canaries' FA Youth Cup-winning side in 1983, jumped straight into the first team the following year. And by the time he was 21 he was the longest-serving player at the club!

"When I look back, I have to admit I probably had too much, too soon. I made my debut when I was just 17 and I'm not sure I was strong enough, mentally or physically, to handle it all," he adds.

"I was in danger of burning myself out and when I got to the end of the 1987-88 season I knew drastic action was needed. It was make or break time as far as my career was concerned.

### Worried man

"I kept reminding myself 'If you don't establish yourself in the first team now, you could be heading down the League to a Third or Fourth Division club'. Yes, I was that worried."

The slimmer, sharper Gordon was a revelation during the 1988-89 campaign as Norwich, rated relegation certainties before the kick-off,

# I ALMOST QUIT NORWICH

# SLIMLINE TONIC SAVED GORDON'S CAREER

completely confounded the critics by setting a hectic pace in the Championship race.

It was only on the last lap that their title challenge faded and The Canaries also celebrated their first FA Cup Semi-Final appearance for 30 years, going down by the only goal to Everton at Villa Park.

And Gordon, whose dazzling wing skills and lethal finishing were a feature of his side's superb form, is very much a reformed character.

"The lads used to call me Flash or Disco," he says with more than a hint of embarrassment. "But those nicknames don't mean a thing now. My idea of a good night out is a quiet meal with Lisa.

"Sure, I still like music and I'm a bit of a fashion freak. But my night-clubbing days are behind me I like to think I'm looking after myself the way a professional sportsman should.

"Lisa deserves a share of any praise I receive. She kept me going on the diet when I felt like weakening!"

Now Gordon is hoping England manager Bobby Robson will forgive and forget an indiscretion by the player during an Under-21 trip to France in the summer of 1987.

Along with his Carrow Road colleague Robert Rosario and Ipswich Town pair Jason Dozzell and Mark Brennan, now with Middlesbrough, he was banned from further international duty after breaking a late-night curfew.

"I've learned my lesson and it will never happen a second time," he maintains.

"The fact that Bobby Robson was prepared to forgive Paul Davis after he was banned for nine games gives me hope he won't ignore me because of what happened in the past."

# DAVID ROCASTLE
## ARSENAL

# TOMMY BURNS
## CELTIC

# QUIZ *MEXICO*

## Complied by Steve Pearce

*The World Cup Finals in Italy are only a few months away. But what can you remember about the last tournament in Mexico four years ago?*

**1** Which Italian was the first player to score in the tournament in the opening game against Bulgaria?

**2** Gary Lineker's hat-trick for England against which country gave Bobby Robson's men a place in the Second Round?

**3** Norman Whiteside scored a goal for Northern Ireland in their group clash with Algeria. What was the result?

**4** Who was stretchered off for Scotland in their 1-0 defeat by Denmark?

**5** Former West Brom winger Carl Valentine represented which nation in the Finals?

**6** How did Hugo Sanchez celebrate his goals in the tournament?

**7** Which African soccer minnows topped Group F?

**8** South Korea's only point of the competition came in a 1-1 draw with who?

**9** Pat Jennings bowed out of the international scene for Northern Ireland against Brazil after making a record number of appearances. How many?

**10** Uruguayan defender Batista challenged Gordon Strachan in the first minute of Scotland's 0-0 draw with their South American opponents. What happened next?

*Emilio Butragueno ... see 20.*

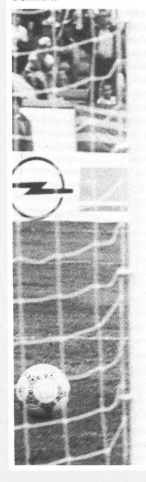

*Uruguayan 'keeper Fernando Alvez was hit for six against Denmark. But who is the player seen here completing his hat-trick?*

# MEMORIES

Answers on page 121

Diego Maradona scored once in his first three matches. Against which country?

**11** Igor Belanov's performances for Russia during the tournament helped him win which prestigious award at the end of the year?

**12** Argentine superstar Diego Maradona scored one goal in his first three matches. Who was it against?

**13** Julio Romero was the star player for which country?

**14** Who knocked out the hosts Mexico in the Quarter-Finals?

**15** Did Michael Laudrup or Preben Elkjaer score a hat-trick for Denmark in their 6-1 thrashing of Uruguay?

**16** Another hat-trick man was Alessandro Altobelli who scored his three for Italy in a 3-2 win against who?

**17** Colin Clarke cracked Northern Ireland's only goal in their 2-1 defeat by Spain after a mistake by which 'keeper?

**18** Which of the following didn't appear on the score sheet in the 1986 World Cup Final? Jose Luis Brown, Karl-Heinz Rummenigge, Olaf Thon and Jorge Burrachaga.

**19** Which former Tottenham star helped Belgium to a thrilling 4-3 victory over Russia?

**20** How many goals did Emilio Butragueno score for Spain in their 5-1 win over Denmark?

**21** Gary Lineker scored six of the seven England goals in the Finals. Who got the other?

**22** Carlos Manuel scored a shock winner for who in a Group F match?

**23** Which Brazilian full-back delighted the crowds with his spectacular goals from long range?

**24** England midfielder Ray Wilkins was sent-off against Morocco for which offence?

**25** Which country was on the wrong end of a 6-0 scoreline against Russia?

**26** Name the Middle East country who were making their first appearance in the Finals?

**27** The Mexican Wave became a popular sight at Football League grounds after being seen by fans following the action in Mexico. What is it?

**28** Who knocked out the holders Italy in the Second Round stage?

**29** What did Luis Fernandez do that ended Brazil's hopes of glory in Mexico?

**30** Which 'keeper was generally regarded as the best in the tournament?

19

# WHATEVER HAPPENED TO ENGLAND'

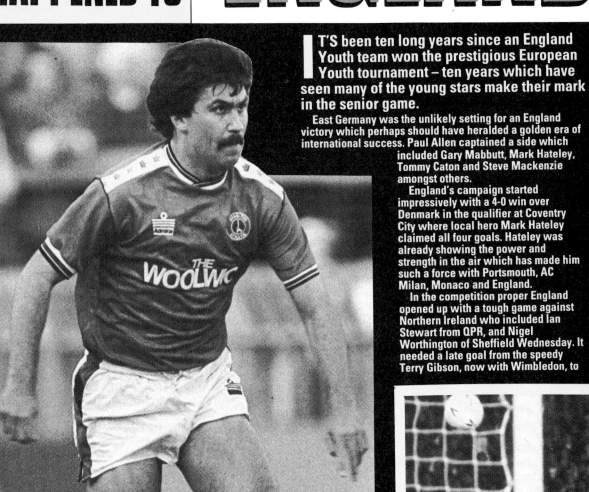

IT'S been ten long years since an England Youth team won the prestigious European Youth tournament – ten years which have seen many of the young stars make their mark in the senior game.

East Germany was the unlikely setting for an England victory which perhaps should have heralded a golden era of international success. Paul Allen captained a side which included Gary Mabbutt, Mark Hateley, Tommy Caton and Steve Mackenzie amongst others.

England's campaign started impressively with a 4-0 win over Denmark in the qualifier at Coventry City where local hero Mark Hateley claimed all four goals. Hateley was already showing the power and strength in the air which has made him such a force with Portsmouth, AC Milan, Monaco and England.

In the competition proper England opened up with a tough game against Northern Ireland who included Ian Stewart from QPR, and Nigel Worthington of Sheffield Wednesday. It needed a late goal from the speedy Terry Gibson, now with Wimbledon, to

# S EURO KINGS?

settle the issue.

The talented Portuguese side were next and provided England with their sternest test of the whole tournament and it needed Steve Mackenzie's powerful shot to secure a 1-1 draw.

By now Mackenzie, who as a 17-year-old signed for Manchester City for £250,000 the previous summer, was warming to his task and his two goals helped England to a comfortable 2-0 win over Yugoslavia before the big match against Holland.

A typical poached effort from Tommy English, from Colchester, ensured victory over the Dutch before the side moved on to the Final against Poland in Leipzig.

The Poles opened the scoring but England remained calm and clinched the game with goals from skipper Paul Allen and Gibson.

The England coach was John Cartwright who guided the Crystal Palace Youth side to successive FA Youth Cup wins in 1977 and 1978.

"It was a team of personalities who slotted together well. Up front Tommy English never strayed far from the

penalty-box, but he was a lethal finisher," said John. "He's still playing at Colchester, but I was disappointed he never progressed further.

"It was a team of personalities who slotted together well. Up front Tommy English never strayed far from the penalty-box, but he was a lethal finisher. He's still playing at Colchester, but I was disappointed he never progressed further.

"Another player I was convinced had a great future was David Barnes, the Coventry full-back. He was big and athletic and gave all the wingers he met a hard time.

"Colin Pates, now at Charlton, was

another strong player who I used as a powerful midfield ball-carrier, the role he played at Chelsea at the time. Obviously up front the strength of Mark Hateley was a tremendous bonus, but the man who made the team tick was Steve Mackenzie.

"I knew Steve well from the Crystal Palace Youth team. He was a really outstanding talent with all the skills. He did well at Manchester City and would have moved on to great things at West Bromwich Albion, but for a terrible groin injury.

England's European victory qualified them for the World Cup in Australia the following Autumn. Many of John's

team were not released by their clubs, but his untried youngsters played superbly to finish a creditable fourth.

Since then John has spent much of his time as senior coach at the Kuwait Sporting Club in the Middle East. He did return briefly to Britain as Don Howe's assistant coach at Arsenal, but resigned along with Howe in the spring of 1986 and returned to Kuwait for another two years.

John certainly knows how to mould young players together. Here for the record is his team which gave England a rare international trophy. Clubs in brackets refer to current or last known clubs of players involved.

TEAM: Mark Kendall (Wolves), Neil Banfield (Crystal Palace, Orient), David Barnes (Swindon Town), Andy Peake (Charlton), Tommy Caton (Charlton), Steve Mackenzie (Charlton), Terry Connor (Portsmouth), Mark Hateley (Monaco), Gary Mabbutt (Tottenham), Paul Allen (Tottenham), Colin Pates (Charlton); Subs Tommy English (Colchester), Terry Gibson (Wimbledon).

"That's not playing the game – open your legs"

"He kicked me first, ref. You can't blame me for retaliating"

"Oops – sorry"

"It always happens when he misses with one of his shoulder-charges"

"Don't worry, boss. Rambo is only showing our new £1 million striker how to score with his head"

"I should stop doing your famous sliding tackles if I were you"

"The ref wants to know if he can have the ball back"

"Will you please inform our golden boy that he's just scored an own goal?"

"I dread sending on our substitute. He seems so accident prone"

# SNAPSHOTS

Charlton's Carl Leaburn reveals how Charlton stayed up for so long ... they get a leg up.

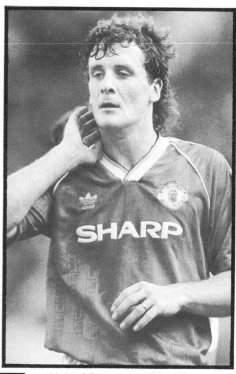

United fans reckon Mark Hughes is magic – but is he really going to pull a rabbit from behind his neck?

John Fashanu is tickled by a remark from the crowd. A fan has asked for The Dons to keep the ball on the deck.

Liverpool's physio Paul Chadwick is on an economy drive. Instead of bandages he collects toilet rolls thrown from The Kop.

Everton's Stuart McCall would have more chance of getting a lift if he went and stood *outside* Goodison Park.

| | | | | |
|---|---|---|---|---|
| ★ 1971-72 | Hereford Utd. | 2 v 1 | Newcastle U |
| ★ 1974-75 | Burnley | 0 v 1 | Wimbledon |
| ★ 1978-75 | Newport Cnty | 2 v 1 | West Ham U. |
| ★ 1988-89 | Sutton Utd. | 2 v 1 | Coventry City |

WHEN the supporters of tiny Sutton United flooded on to the Gander Green Lane pitch last January after their team's remarkable FA Cup conquest of First Division Coventry City, they were right to throw themselves wholeheartedly into the moment of triumph.

Three other ties in particular, over the last 20 years, illustrate how fortunes can fluctuate after a major Cup shock.

Southern League Hereford United, under player-manager Colin Addison were the surprise team of the 1971-72 competition.

They knocked out First Division Newcastle United – Malcolm Macdonald and all – in a Third Round replay, after a 2-2 draw at St. James's.

Ronnie Radford's spectacular solo effort to equalise at Edgar Street is one of the most shown goals in FA Cup history. It earned the underdogs extra-time and the chance to snatch a sensational winner by Ricky George.

# CUP SHOCKERS

*Sutton's Matthew Hanlan grabs the winner against Coventry in 1989.*

# When giants were toppled by the minnows

**Above: All conquering heroes Hereford mobbed by the fans. Right: Wimbledon with the FA Cup after toppling the mighty Liverpool.**

Four months after that stirring performance, Hereford won long-overdue entry into the Football League, taking Barrow's place.

They certainly made the most of their shock victory over Newcastle, winning first time promotion to Division Three, and by 1976 they were in the Second Division.

Newcastle, six times FA Cup winners were none the worse for their humiliating defeat and, two years later reached another Wembley Final.

## Sensation

When Wimbledon beat First Division Burnley 1-0 at Turf Moor in the Third Round in 1975, they created more than that season's Cup sensation. For the respective fortunes of the two clubs, following Mick Mahon's 49th minute winner represent a remarkable contrast.

Wimbledon, then in the Southern League, went on to establish themselves as the country's top non-League side and were admitted to the Football League in 1977. The rest – a meteoric climb to the First Division and a 1988 FA Cup triumph – is history.

For Burnley, however, life has been so different. In 1976 they dropped out of the top flight, beginning the slide that was to take them down to Division Four.

But perhaps the saddest reversal of fortune after FA Cup glory concerned Newport County. In 1979, as a Fourth Division side, they overcame Second Division pace-setters West Ham United.

When Eddie Woods headed their 81st minute winner at Somerton Park, they seemed to be on the verge of good times. Indeed, for years after that victory Newport battled gamely on, even reaching the European Cup-Winners' Cup quarter-final in 1981.

But financial problems were never far away. At the end of season 1987-88 County dropped out of the Football League and into the GM Vauxhall Conference. By the following March, they were out of business, finally beaten by debts of £126,000.

West Ham, of course, recovered from that Cup shock at Newport. They won the Cup for the third time in 1980, and returned to the First Division a year later.

How interesting it will be in ten or 15 years' time to reflect on the fortunes of Sutton and Coventry. Will Sutton "do a Wimbledon"?

Will Coventry, Cup-winners for the first time in 1987, have sampled further glory?

The FA Cup poses that sort of question every season. What will it be this time?

# The Doc's verdict

£1m

A NEW AGE dawned in soccer in February 1979 when Trevor Francis became the first British player to be transferred for £1 million, moving to Nottingham Forest from Birmingham City.

Since then, up to last season's deadline, there have been another 30 transfers involving British stars which topped the million pound barrier.

One man who has watched the transfer dealings with great interest over the years is Tommy Docherty. The Doc gives SHOOT his verdict on the million-pound buys and a value-for-money rating.

**IAN RUSH** – Liverpool to Juventus £3.2m, June 1987. Juventus to Liverpool – £2.8m, August 1988.
He has not been so successful since his return to Anfield from Juventus, but I believe his best is still to come.
**Verdict: 9 out of 10 – A HIT.**

Gary Lineker

Richard Gough

**GARY LINEKER** – Leicester City to Everton – £1.1m, June 1985. Everton to Barcelona – £2.75m, June 1986.
An outstanding success. He conducts himself magnificently. Gary is a great goalscorer who works very hard for the team.
**Verdict: 9 out of 10 – A HIT.**

**TONY COTTEE** – West Ham to Everton – £2.2m, July 1988.
Has had an excellent partner in Graeme Sharp, but has not scored as many goals as he should.
**Verdict: 6 out of 10 – A MISS.**

**MARK HUGHES** – Man Utd to Barcelona – £2.3m, May 1986. Barcelona to Man Utd – £1.8m, June 1988.
Mark shouldn't have been sold in the first place, but is playing twice as well since his return. Possibly the best centre forward in the game at the moment.
**Verdict: 9 out of 10 – A HIT.**

**PAUL GASCOIGNE** – Newcastle Utd to Tottenham – £2m, July 1987.
A hit with the media, he still needs to play as well as he talks about his game. Has the ability to improve.
**Verdict: 5 out of 10 – A MISS.**

**PETER BEARDSLEY** – Newcastle Utd to Liverpool – £1.9m, July 1987.
Outstanding. He was great at Newcastle and is great at Liverpool. Could walk into any team.
**Verdict: 9 out of 10 – A HIT.**

**PAUL STEWART** – Man City to Tottenham – £1.7m, June 1988.
Found things more difficult at Spurs. He could eventually do it. I'm hopeful of improvement.
**Verdict: 6 out of 10 – A MISS.**

**BRYAN ROBSON** – WBA to Man Utd – £1.5m, October 1981.
Over the years at Old Trafford, a tremendous hit. And last season was his best season ever.
**Verdict: 11 out of 10 – A HIT.**

**RAY WILKINS** – Man Utd to AC Milan – £1.5m, June 1984.
A tremendous professional. A big success both here and in Italy and he is still playing well for Rangers. Great managerial material.
**Verdict: 9 out of 10 – A HIT.**

**RICHARD GOUGH** – Tottenham to Rangers – £1.5m, October 1987.
A fine player who looks so good on the ball. Richard has played well for Scotland, Spurs and Rangers.
**Verdict: 9 out of 10 – A HIT.**

**ANDY GRAY** – Aston Villa to Wolves – £1,469,000, September 1979.
Didn't do well at Wolves, but he had a lot of injury trouble.
**Verdict: 6 out of 10 – A MISS.**

**STEVE DALEY** – Wolves to Man City – £1,437,500, September 1979.
Perhaps the biggest transfer disaster of them all! He played just 48 games for City before going to America.
**Verdict: 3 out of 10 – A MISS.**

**KENNY SANSOM** – Crystal Palace to Arsenal for £1.35m, August 1980.
I never thought of him as a great defender, but Arsenal certainly got good service for their money. Good buy for Newcastle.
**Verdict: 8 out of 10 – A HIT.**

**KEVIN REEVES** – Norwich City to Man City – £1.25m, March 1980.
He found the step up in class from a country club too difficult.
**Verdict: 5 out of 10 – A MISS.**

**IAN WALLACE** – Coventry City to Nottingham Forest – £1.25m, July 1980.
He scored the goals for Coventry, but just couldn't do it at Forest. Moved to the French club Brest.
**Verdict: 5 out of 10 – A MISS.**

**CLIVE ALLEN** – QPR to Arsenal – £1.2m, June 1980. Arsenal to Crystal Palace – £1.25m, August 1980. Tottenham to Bordeaux – £1m, May 1988.
Has scored goals wherever he has gone. Why he has not been in the England team more often, I just don't know?
**Verdict: 9 out of 10 – A HIT.**

**GARRY BIRTLES** – Nottingham Forest to Man Utd – £1.25m, October 1980.
He was one of the biggest misses of them all. I never saw him as being worth that sort of money. He was never a prolific goalscorer.
**Verdict: 5 out of 10 – A MISS.**

**TREVOR FRANCIS** – Birmingham City to Nottingham Forest for £1.18m, Feb 1979. Forest to Man City for £1.2m, September 1981.
He never fulfilled his potential, in my view. I always thought of him as a nearly man, although he was injured a lot.
**Verdict: 6 out of 10 – A MISS.**

**FRANK McAVENNIE** – Celtic to West Ham – £1.25m, March 1989.
He was a great success in his first season with West Ham. I predict he will be a big hit with The Hammers again.
**Verdict: 9 out of 10 – A HIT.**

**JUSTIN FASHANU** – Norwich to Nottingham Forest – £1m, August 1981.
A great disappointment. He had looked a very good player at Norwich. Just didn't settle at Forest.
**Verdict: 5 out of 10 – A MISS.**

*Above: Paul Gascoigne – still to prove himself but the talent is there. Below: Monaco's Mark Hateley.*

**LUTHER BLISSETT** – Watford to AC Milan – £1m, June 1983.
A tremendous goalscorer. Was difficult for him in Italy because the game is very defensive there and didn't suit him.
**Verdict: 7 out of 10 – A MISS IN ITALY, A HIT HERE.**

**STEVE ARCHIBALD** – Tottenham to Barcelona – £1m, July, 1984.
He did it in Scotland and in Spain. A success. A great finisher.
**Verdict: 8 out of 10 – A HIT.**

**MARK HATELEY** – AC Milan to Monaco – £1m, June 1987.
Mark did well at Coventry and Portsmouth. Won a Championship medal with Monaco, making him an outstanding success.
**Verdict: 9 out of 10 – A HIT.**

**GARY STEVENS** – Everton to Rangers – £1m, July 1988.
I thought he was a better player two or three years ago. One million pounds is a lot of money to pay for a full-back.
**Verdict: 7 out of 10 – A HIT.**

**DEAN SAUNDERS** – Oxford United to Derby County – £1m, October 1988.
A lot of money for a relatively unknown player. A good goalscorer.
**Verdict: 7 out of 10 – A HIT.**

**So there it is. The Doc's thoughts on the big money men. And Tom has some strong words to say on the state of the transfer market generally:**
"Some players are being bought for silly money. But if you want the merchandise you have to pay the fee," he says.

# Top 'keepers recall the

# VILLIANS

**A** goalkeeper can quickly turn the cheers in to boos. A series of brilliant saves are soon forgotten if he lets a goal slip in through his legs.

Here SHOOT talks to some of Britain's top 'keepers about the worst and best goals that they have conceded.

**DAVE BEASANT:** In his last game for Wimbledon he saved a penalty in the FA Cup Final. His debut was a disaster though:
*Worst goal:* It came against Blackpool when Wimbledon were in the Third Division, on my debut as a League professional. Colin Morris hit an average shot but when I stooped to pull the ball into my chest it slipped straight through my hands and under my legs. The ball stopped one foot over the goal line. We lost 2-1.
*Best goal:* It was by Dave Phillips, of Manchester City. A low cross came in, someone dummied it and Phillips came racing in and shot first time from the edge of the area. The ball flew into the corner and I was still thinking of diving as it went past me.

**DAVE SEAMAN:** QPR's £1 million rated 'keeper:
*Worst goal:* When Peterborough were playing York City. I threw the ball out,

*Dave Beasant*

*Dave Seaman prevents a Manchester United goal in the Cup Third Round replay at Old Trafford.*

# moments they became

## and HEROES

straight to one of their forwards. He controlled it on his chest, came straight back at me and slipped it through my legs.
*Best goal:* The best scored against me was by Bryan Robson, in last season's F.A. Cup Third Round, second replay at Old Trafford. He controlled the ball on the edge of the area. Then he hit it with the outside of his left, straight into the top corner.

**BRYAN GUNN,** who joined Norwich from Aberdeen in October 1986:
*Worst goal:* Norwich were playing Everton at Goodison Park. I raced out to clear Trevor Putney's back pass, tried to nutmeg their forward and failed. I brought him down and they scored from the penalty.

*Best goal:* By Siggi Jonsson, of Sheffield Wednesday. He shot from about 35 yards out; it was an unstoppable drive.

**TONY COTON:** Watford's 'keeper saved a penalty on his League debut for Birmingham, but reveals here, some less fortunate moments.
*Worst goal:* It was a free-kick scored by Mark Ward of West Ham. I had saved an identical one from him earlier. This time the ball slipped through my hands and legs, for a goal.
*Best goal:* Ian Rush has scored a lot of good goals against me. When you're preparing for a shot from the edge of the area, Liverpool switch the play with one quick pass. Rushie always seemed to be on the other flank to finish it.

Tony Coton

*Sheffield Wednesday's Siggi Jonsson (11) belts an unstoppable drive past Bryan Gunn.*

"Stay calm lads, if there's a dog on the pitch I'll shoo it off, OK?"

# FACE THE ST★RS

Our unkind layout artists have hidden the faces of these three First and Second Division stars. Can you identify the mystery men?

ANSWERS ON PAGE 121

**1** A defender who joined his present club from QPR.

**2** Hard tackling midfield skipper of The Lions.

**3** Former Old Trafford star now at Ayresome Park.

# GORAM'S KICKING HIS WAY TO SUCCESS

**H**is accent may be pure Coronation Street but it was taking the tartan trail to Scotland that launched Andy Goram on the road to international stardom.

The Bury-born goalkeeper moved North of the border in October, 1987, when ambitious Premier Division outfit Hibs forked out £320,00 to lure him away from Oldham Athletic.

"No disrespect to Oldham and the English Second Division, but there's no doubt that coming to Scotland and playing with and against better players has improved my game," he maintains.

But it was during his spell with The Latics that the 25-year-old 'keeper made the international breakthrough – and Boundary Park boss Joe Royle played a key role.

Goram had been earning rave reports when Royle picked up the phone in his office to call Scotland manager Alex Ferguson, who had just inherited the reins following the sudden death of former supremo Jock Stein.

"Three days later I had a call from Fergie telling me he'd be in touch," recalls Goram. "He certainly kept his word because I was named in his next squad and won my first cap when I came on as substitute against East Germany at Hampden."

## Thrashed

Goram did well enough to be given a full 90 minutes as the Scots thrashed Rumania 3-0 at Hampden and again when they held the highly-rated Dutch to a 0-0 draw in Eindhoven.

His displays earned him a place in Scotland's squad for the Mexico-hosted World Cup and he seems certain to be involved again if the Scots book a fifth consecutive Finals ticket to Italy in 1990.

Not surprisingly, Goram was linked with a number of big-money English clubs before deciding to follow in his father's footsteps and join Hibs.

Lewis Goram, also a goalkeeper, was on the Easter Road payroll between 1948 and 1950 but did not influence his son's decision.

"Having made the breakthrough into the Scotland squad while still at Oldham, I saw the move to Edinburgh as a terrific opportunity to enhance my international career," says Andy.

"I figured Andy Roxburgh would be able to keep a closer eye on me. With Hibs, I'm finally in the limelight and that's got to be to my advantage."

Goram's dedication will benefit club and country for years to come. Long after his colleagues have left the training pitch he devotes overtime to his kicking.

It has already paid dividends – he scored in his first season with Hibs against Morton! – and he adds: "I don't just go for length. The kicks have to be accurate, too.

"I put up markers in different areas of the pitch and if I don't hit the target seven times out of ten I just keep going until I do!"

Goram actually launched his career when he joined West Bromwich Albion straight from school, but shortly after manager Ron Atkinson quit to join Manchester United.

New boss Ronnie Allen handed the young 'keeper a free transfer and Goram admits: "I thought that was the end. I never thought I'd get another chance until Oldham made me an offer."

# Neil Orr

## HIBERNIAN

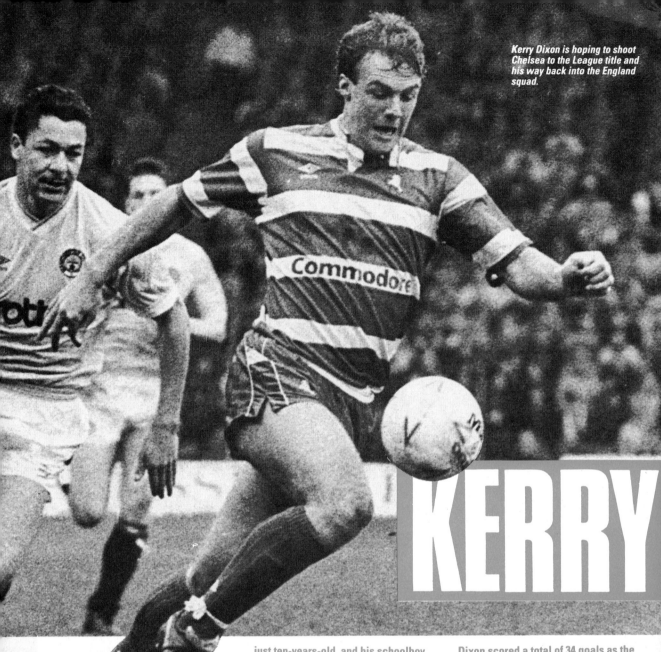

# KERRY

**K**erry Dixon's career has enveloped more ups 'n' downs than a roller-coaster ride.

And the blond Chelsea striker hopes the club's return to the First Division has put it back on the upward scale, with an England recall somewhere along the ride.

Dixon, now 28, has been scoring goals since he was knee high to Charlie Cooke. His instinct was spotted by home-town club Luton when he was just ten-years-old, and his schoolboy exploits once brought him 13 goals in one game, and around 150 goals in a season.

But heartbreak was soon to follow. Luton finally decided they weren't going to sign him as a professional and, soon after, so did Tottenham after playing him in their youth team for a season.

So Dixon was forced to find a job as an apprentice toolmaker while scoring goals for fun with Chesham United and Dunstable.

But his perseverance was to pay off. Maurice Evans, then manager of Reading, took a gamble that was to pay handsome dividends for both the club and the player.

Dixon struck 51 goals in 116 League games for The Royals, and won the SHOOT/adidas Golden Shoe Award for leading the Third Division goalscoring list before his £175,000 transfer to Chelsea in 1983.

In his first season at Stamford Bridge Dixon scored a total of 34 goals as the club won the Second Division Championship. Twenty eight of those goals came in League action, earning him another Golden Shoe.

Then, in his first season in Division One, Dixon completed a remarkable hat-trick when he finished as top scorer with 24 League goals – 36 in total.

## England debut

Three Golden Shoes and a total of 103 League goals in 199 games was a record England manager Bobby Robson could not ignore.

Dixon made his full international debut for England, after a scoring debut for the Under-21's and a brief substitute appearance for the seniors against Mexico, in Mexico City in June 1985. West Germany were the opponents, and Dixon made an encouraging start, creating a goalscoring chance for captain Bryan Robson.

That was just the start. In the second half the Chelsea ace scored twice to ease England to a 3-0 victory.

When Dixon scored two more in his next appearance four days later against the USA in Los Angeles, it seemed he was set to carry his superb goalscoring record on to the international scene.

But three more starts, plus another two as a substitute, failed to produce any more goals. Dixon was dropped from Robson's squad after England's friendly defeat in Sweden in 1986.

## Crash!

"And I deserved it," he admits. "At the time my form had dipped and Chelsea were beginning to struggle in the First Division."

After several years climbing the roller-coaster, Dixon's career came crashing. The turning point can be pinpointed exactly – a serious stomach injury sustained in January 1986.

It happened during the opening minutes of a televised FA Cup-tie against Liverpool, and Dixon recalls: "It was a serious injury and it took me a long time to recover.

"I tore the stomach muscle, a sort of bubble formed, there was internal bleeding and the movement around my midriff was completely restricted.

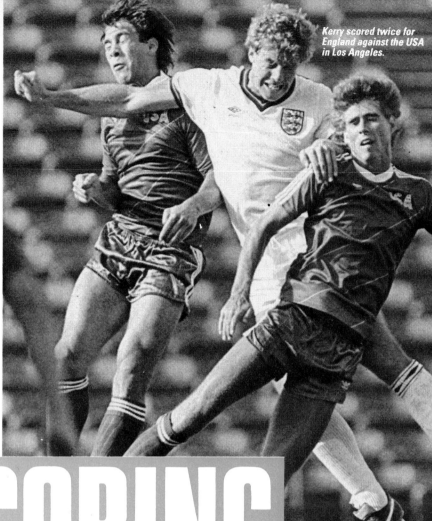

Kerry scored twice for England against the USA in Los Angeles.

# ON SCORING

Gordon Durie.

"My next match after the injury was for England in Israel, which was a ridiculous situation really. I knew as soon as the game had started that I wasn't anywhere near match fit and consequently I wasn't able to do myself justice."

As Dixon's form dipped so did the fortunes of Chelsea. From January 1986 through to May 1988 Dixon scored just 23 goals in 82 games and The Blues were relegated to the Second Division.

But there was plenty of heartbreak for Dixon outside the penalty box during those not-so-sweet 16 months. He was unable to escape from the bitter feuding inside Stamford Bridge, and had several bust-ups with manager of the time John Hollins.

So when a £1.2 million transfer to Arsenal seemed on the cards Dixon was naturally anxious to find sanctuary away from the Bridge of Sighs.

But the move was scuppered by the club's chairman Ken Bates and the player was resigned to reluctantly seeing out his contract.

Dixon's roller-coaster career was to take an upward swing before that, however, to such epic proportions that he agreed a new four year contract before the end of the season.

New manager Bobby Campbell had been unable to stop the club's slide into Division Two, but he restored confidence and rebuilt team spirit with such stunning effect that Dixon was happy to pledge his future to the club.

Last season Chelsea finished the season as Second Division Champions while setting a new points record.

Dixon was back among the goals again, and seems set to terrorise First Division defences in 1990.

George Graham's patience finally paid off on the last game of last season when Arsenal grabbed the League Championship with virtually the final kick of the campaign. The Arsenal boss' reluctance to spend millions in the transfer market brought a wave of criticism but Graham's perseverance with his young side brought its rewards in dramatic fashion at Anfield. Liverpool, needing to avoid a two goal defeat to win the title, were odds on favourites. But Alan Smith opened Arsenal's account early in the second-half and Michael Thomas scored a last gasp winner to take the crown to Highbury.

# GUNNERS

*Tony Adams, Steve Bould and David O'Leary celebrate the Championship.*

# GLORY

Michael Thomas scores Arsenal's Championship winner at Anfield.

WE'VE WON THE CUP!

Alan Smith topped the First Division goalcharts with 23 last season.

# RANGER

R angers stormed to their second Championship under the leadership of Graeme Souness as the Premier League felt the full force of the multi million men from Ibrox. Souness' big money signings Kevin Drinkell, Gary Stevens and Mel Sterland all revelled in front of the regular 40,000 crowds as the Light Blues led the title race from start to finish. What must be worrying for their opponents is the fact that the Glasgow club seem to have an endless supply of money and look set to dominate the Scottish scene for years to come. What price Souness picking up his third title this season?

*Kevin Drinkell was Rangers' top scorer in the League with 11 goals.*

**We are the ★ Champions**

*Skipper Terry Butcher leads his team on a lap of honour after their 4-0 win over Hearts had given them the title.*

# S RULE

The Premier League Champions with the trophy... the second under Souness.

The wing wizardry of Mark Walters made him a firm favourite with the Ibrox crowd.

Graeme Souness

# DOUBLE DIAMONDS

## Ace Ally tames Dons

**WE'VE WON THE CUP!**

**A**lly McCoist was the toast of Rangers when his double strike helped the Ibrox club retain the Skol Cup last season with a thrilling 3-2 win over Aberdeen at Hampden. The Scottish striker tucked a penalty past Theo Snelders for Rangers' first and, after Ian Ferguson and Davie Dodds with two for the Dons had tied the scores up at 2-2, Ally struck in the final minute to give Graeme Souness' men their third successive Skol Cup triumph.

*Ferguson and McCoist celebrate after Rangers' grandstand finish finally saw off Aberdeen's challenge.*

*The winner. Ally strikes in the closing stages to win the Cup for the Ibrox side.*

Nottingham Forest – 1989 Littlewoods Cup winners.

# Clough tops the Hatters

**T**hey came to acclaim Brian Clough's managerial wizardry and left remembering the performance of a sensational striker – the Nottingham Forest manager's son Nigel. The England international grabbed the headlines from his famous father with a two goal display that destroyed Luton in last season's Littlewoods Cup Final. The Hatters led through a Mick Harford header but young Clough kept his nerve to equalise with a penalty, Neil Webb put them ahead and Nigel cracked Forest's third to give his dad his first major honour in nine years.

Nigel holds off Luton's Tim Breacker in his match winning performance for his dad's side.

Aldridge puts Liverpool ahead with his first touch after four minutes.

Skipper Ronnie Whelan get his hands on the FA Cup.

# GOAL

## Super sub Ian snatches FA Cup for Reds

Ian Rush emerged from the sub's bench to become the FA Cup Final hero for Liverpool. The lethal striker replaced John Aldridge, who had opened The Reds' account after four minutes, in the closing stages of normal time, Liverpool led 1-0 until the final minute when Everton sub Stuart McCall equalised. Rushie put Kenny Dalglish's men ahead in extra-time, McCall drew Everton level again but the Welshman was at hand to head the Anfield men to Wembley glory.

## WE'VE WON THE CUP!

Rushie gives Liverpool a 2-1 lead in extra-time, firing past Neville Southall.

# RUSH

The winner. Rush strikes again with this deft header to give The Reds a 3-2 win and the FA Cup.

# MILLER

## Little Joe grabs glory for Celtic

WE'VE WON THE CUP!

# MAGIC

**J**oe Miller turned Rangers' dream of landing the treble in Scotland into a nightmare as Celtic won the Scottish Cup with a lone goal from their winger. Little Joe seized on a mistake from Rangers full-back Gary Stevens and left 'keeper Chris Woods with no chance (below) to give Billy McNeill's men their only trophy in last season's campaign.

# EUROPE'S ELITE

**I**taly reigned in the battle of the European club scene last season with representatives in each of the three Finals. Sampdoria's defeat by Barcelona in the European Cup-Winners' Cup was quickly forgotten as Diego Maradona's Napoli won the UEFA Cup at the expense of West Germans VfB Stuttgart and AC Milan thrashed Steaua Bucharest 4-0 in the European Cup Final.

Gary Lineker helped Barcelona to Cup-Winners' Cup victory over Sampdoria

Diego Maradona inspired Napoli to their first European triumph with the Italian club beating Stuttgart 5-4 over two legs.

**WE'VE WON THE CUP!**

The Dutch destroyer, Ruud Gullit holds aloft the European Cup.

Gullit strikes to give AC Milan the lead in their emphatic victory over Steaua Bucharest.

PHILIPS

# ALL SQUARED UP

Use the clues given to help you identify these four stars from the English First Division and Scottish Premier League.

Answers on page 121.

1 Born in Glasgow, plays his football in Liverpool and has represented Eire?

2 Former West Ham striker who is now earning his money at the Baseball Ground.

3 Led Norwich's midfield last season after joining the club from Burnley.

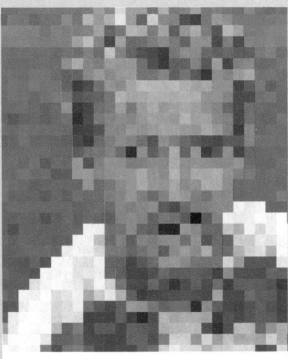

4 Experienced Celtic defender who has won eight international caps with Scotland.

**D**undee boss Gordon Wallace knows all about the great divide on Tayside.

He was born and brought up in the city, followed both teams as a youngster and has been on the payroll at Dens Park and Tannadice as player, coach and manager.

Wallace knows better than most that while both grounds are in the same street – only 200 yards separates the respective main entrances – they are miles apart when it comes to rivalry on the terraces.

His task is to turn back the clock to the days when Dundee reigned supreme on Tayside and neighbours Dundee United were very much the poor relations.

It was Wallace the striker who earned the Dark Blues their last major honour, when he scored the only goal at Hampden in 1973 to lift the League Cup at the expense of firm favourites Celtic.

Now that he's in charge at the club where he scored the bulk of his 300 senior goals, Wallace is determined to

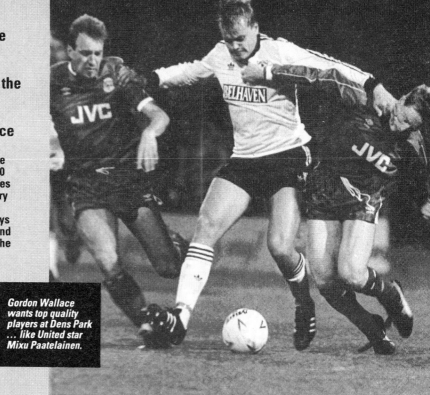

Gordon Wallace wants top quality players at Dens Park ... like United star Mixu Paatelainen.

# I ENVY UNITED

## admits Dundee boss

recapture the glory days by taking a leaf out of United's book.

He was right hand man to Tannadice supremo Jim McLean for six years before being lured across the road again. And he admits: "If I could achieve only a fraction of what has been achieved by United I'd be a success.

"I don't mind admitting I'm envious of United. I left a tremendous set-up to become a manager and I would love to think that one day I can build Dundee to a similar high standard.

"But that type of success doesn't come easy, as I know Jim McLean would be the first to admit. I was under no illusions when I accepted the job. I fully realised the magnitude of the task."

Wallace became Dundee's fourth manager in three years, following Archie Knox, Jocky Scott and Dave Smith, who quit just seven months after leaving Plymouth to take charge in the summer of 1988.

He wasn't helped when star striker Tommy Coyne, who had cost a mere £70,000 when signed from Dundee United just over two years earlier, was transferred to Celtic in a club record

£500,000 deal.

But Wallace points out: "Sometimes you have no choice but to release players to finance other things, like the purchase of new faces or putting the youth policy into top gear.

"You only have to look at what's happened across the road to appreciate the value of a decent youth policy. The United squad is littered with players picked up straight from school.

"We must aim to do the same, not only from Tayside but the whole of Scotland. But to put a scheme into operation costs money and it takes a few years to bear fruit.

"I don't like to tell supporters to be patient, because I know how desperate they are to be part of a successful club, but I think they know it will take time to get things going the way we want."

# CROSSWORD

## A

See 12 across.

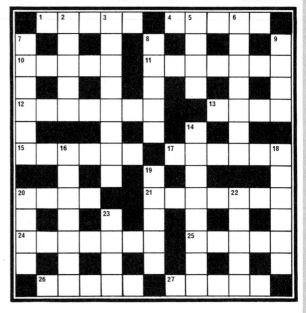

### CLUES ACROSS:–
(1) Nicky – , Middlesbrough defender. (5)
(4) Liam – , West Ham midfielder. (5)
(10) Lined up – as for a shot at goal. (5)
(11) "The Gunners" from Highbury. (7)
(12) John – , Newcastle United striker. (7)
(13) If Swansea, Bournemouth, Doncaster & Everton give "NEAR"; what do Stoke, Wigan, Derby & Clydebank give? (4)
(15) Bryan – , Manchester United skipper. (6)
(17) John – , Luton Town defender. (6)
(20) Assess the current form of a player. (4)
(21) Adrian – , Plymouth defender. (7)
(24) Steve – , Nottingham Forest defender. (7)
(25) Paul –, Tottenham midfielder. (5)
(26) The 8th, 4th, 6th, 7th & 5th letters of "THE SEAGULLS" (Brighton). (5)
(27) David – , Manchester City midfield player. (5)

### CLUES DOWN:–
(2) Russell – , Southampton defender. (5)
(3) John – , Newcastle defender. (8)
(5) LEROY - - - -NIOR, West Ham striker. (4)
(6) Mal – , Manchester United defender. (7)
(7) GLENN PENNY- - - - - -, Crystal Palace midfielder. (6)
(8) Martin – , striker for 11 Across. (5)
(9) Morton's colours are – and white hoops. (4)
(14) Scottish Division Two club from Gayfield Park. (8)
(16) Surname of Spurs defender. (6)
(18) Going up – as a ball soaring over the crossbar. (6)
(19) – Stadium; ground of Cambridge United. (5)
(20) Brian – Nottm. Forest midfielder. (4)
(22) A young Sheffield Wednesday fan, perhaps. (5)
(23) "THE - - - - S" nickname of Mansfield Town. (4)

## B

### CLUES ACROSS:–
(1) Richard – , Luton winger. (5)
(4) The 1st, 2nd, 10th & 8th letters of CHESTERFIELD. (4)
(10) Steve – , Liverpool defender. (5)
(11) Roy – , Luton Town ace striker. (7)
(12) Division Four club of whom one nickname is "Turfites". (7)
(13) If Cardiff, Chelsea, Everton & Reading give "FANG"; what do Watford, Bury, Clyde & Leeds give? (4)
(15) – Road, ground of Leeds United. (6)
(17) London club from Craven Cottage. (6)
(20) One side of the field of play. (4)
(21) – Road; ground of Liverpool. (7)
(24) – ground of Barnsley. (7)
(25) The 2nd, 6th, 5th, 8th & 10th letters of ROMEO ZONDERVAN. (5)
(26) PAUL - - - -OUT, Southampton striker. (4)
(27) Liam – , West Ham midfielder. (5)

### CLUES DOWN:–
(2) "Happen" from the initial letters of Coventry City, Rangers & Oxford United. (5)
(3) Brian – , Coventry City defender. (8)
(5) - - - -BURY; home of "The Gunners". (4)
(6) Mike – , Derby County defender. (7)
(7) The 7th, 11th, 2nd, 1st, 4th & 14th letters of BALLYMENA UNITED. (6)
(8) Games played on opponent's grounds. (5)
(9) – Park; home ground of Dundee. (4)
(14) Lancashire ground of 12 Across. (4 & 4)
(16) Gary – , England striker. (7)
(18) Lawrie – , Sheffield Wednesday defender. (6)
(19) Bryan – , Manchester City defender. (5)
(20) Paul – , Brighton stiker. (4)
(22) – Park; ground of Blackburn Rovers. (5)
(23) Surname of Queens Park Rangers veteran. (4)

See 11 across

50

# SPOT THE DIFFERENCE

Our artist has made ten changes to the picture. Can you find them?

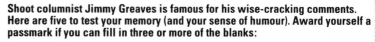
"Talk about players off with injuries ... that's the Chairman!"

## TRIVIA
### TRUE OR FALSE

England goalkeeper Peter Shilton was worried that his arms were not long enough to be a world-class 'keeper so he used to spend hours stretching them by hanging from the bannisters at his home. True or false?

## JUST AMAZING

Cardiff City trainer Ron Durban resigned from his job in 1974 in strange circumstances. He was accused of pouring a bucket of water over a York City fan's head during a heated touchline argument.

## Flashback
### FACT OR FICTION

Arsenal striker Charlie George was booked for running a time-wasting lap of honour in celebration of his winning goal for Arsenal in the 1971 FA Cup Final against Liverpool. True or false?

# GREAVSIEISMS

Shoot columnist Jimmy Greaves is famous for his wise-cracking comments. Here are five to test your memory (and your sense of humour). Award yourself a passmark if you can fill in three or more of the blanks:

1. ................ smoked so many cigarettes during the World Cup matches that he should have carried a Government health warning.

2. ................keep the ball in the air so much that they should be sponsored by a satellite television company.

3. ................ has eaten so many *Mars* Bars that he is sure to be successful whether he's going to work, rest or play.

4. ................is being treated diabolically by the tabloid press as if he's a murderer. I reckon I would become one if they wrote that sort of thing about me.

5. ................ always looks as miserable as a man down to his last penny rather than the manager of the best team in the land.

# RAY OF THE RANGERS

RAY AND A COUPLE OF TEAMMATES WERE RELAXING WITH A GAME OF GOLF THE DAY BEFORE A BIG GAME...

WHACK!

RAY DROVE OFF...

OOPS! I'VE SLICED THAT!

THE BALL SMACKED INTO THE TREES AND REBOUNDED...

POW! PING! WHOOSH! POW! ZIP!

...KNOCKING POOR RAY ON THE BONCE!

DONK!

ARE YOU OKAY, RAY?

YEAH-SURE! LET'S TAKE A SHOWER AND CALL IT A DAY!

AFTER THE SHOWER...

ER, RAY, WHY'VE YOU GOT YOUR UNDERPANTS ON YOUR HEAD?

'COS IT MIGHT RAIN, OF COURSE! SEE YOU TOMORROW!

NEXT DAY AT THE GROUND THE MANAGER WAS WORRIED...

5 MINUTES TO KICK-OFF AND STILL NO SIGN OF RAY!

HOME TEAM

HIYA FOLKS - SORRY I'M LATE - COULDN'T DO A THING WITH MY HAIR!

EEK!

SCRIPT: TONY HUSBAND
ART: STEVE NEGARRY

# TOP CATS

**W**ould you dive head first at a striker's feet or stand in the way of a bullet strike from point blank range? The crazy men of football do. Here SHOOT spotlights five of the best 'keepers in the business – men who have really proved they are top cats.

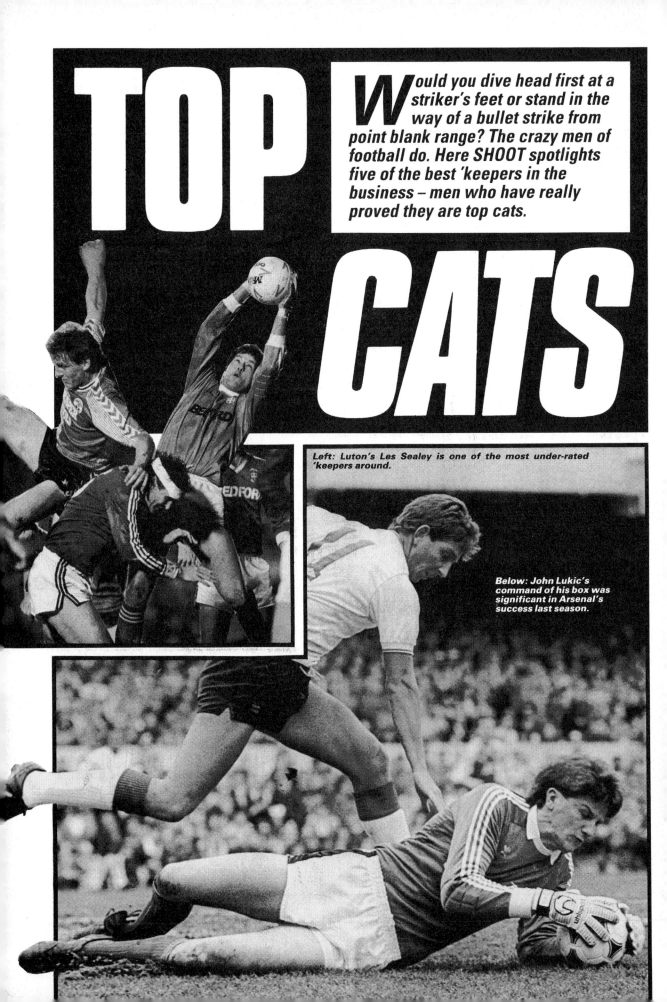

*Left: Luton's Les Sealey is one of the most under-rated 'keepers around.*

*Below: John Lukic's command of his box was significant in Arsenal's success last season.*

*The king – Derby and England star Peter Shilton saves superbly from Arsenal's Paul Merson.*

*Aberdeen's Theo Snelders – the current Players' Player of the Year in Scotland.*

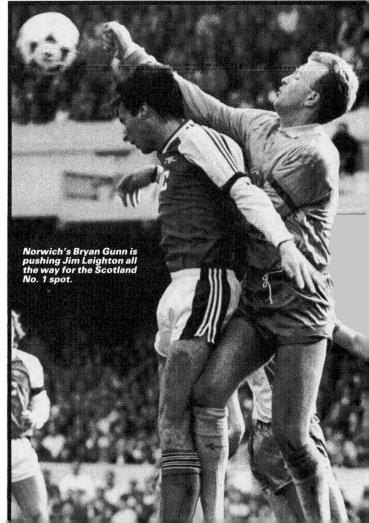

*Norwich's Bryan Gunn is pushing Jim Leighton all the way for the Scotland No. 1 spot.*

# AWAY THE LA

## Newcastle's

**E**ngland manager Bobby Robson was linked with the Newcastle job, but stayed away from the North East to make his managerial name at Ipswich.

● Republic of Ireland manager Jack Charlton, walked out on Newcastle because fans gave him so much stick.

● John Burridge (Southampton). Born Workington, Cumbria, an obvious catchment area for Newcastle United. But he made his name at Aston Villa.

● Neil Aspin (Leeds United). Born Gateshead, Newcastle. But moved straight to boyhood heroes Leeds.

● Barry Venison (Liverpool). Born Consett, N.E. Chose Sunderland instead of Newcastle.

● Steve Bruce (Manchester United). Born Newcastle. But took the familiar route South to find League football with Gillingham and stardom at Norwich.

● Andy Linighan (Norwich). Born Hartlepool, N.E. Described by Tony Cascarino as the "best in the country" but slipped through Magpie net.

● Kevin Richardson (Arsenal). Born Newcastle. Turned down Newcastle for "Bigger welcome" at Everton.

● Bryan Robson (Manchester United and England captain). Born Chester Le Street. Moved away from N.E. to begin his professional career at West Bromwich Albion.

● Paul Gascoigne (Spurs and England). Born Gateshead,

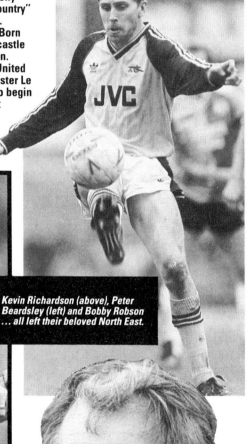

Kevin Richardson (above), Peter Beardsley (left) and Bobby Robson ... all left their beloved North East.

# DS!

# lost team

*Former Newcastle star Chris Waddle (white shirt), takes on Bryan Robson.*

Newcastle. Left after rows with import Mirandinha for more ambitious White Hart Lane set-up.

● Peter Beardsley (Liverpool and England). Born Newcastle. But moved across to start his career with Carlisle. Later set Geordies alight with Keegan.

● Alan Shearer (Southampton). Born Newcastle. A star of the future already made impact on First Division, another Geordie lost to South.

● Chris Waddle (Spurs and England). Another Geordie born and bred who didn't want to stay. Says: "Newcastle lacked ambition."

● Kevin Dillon (Portsmouth). Born Sunderland.

● Graham Shaw (Stoke). Born Newcastle.

AND THERE ARE MORE.

For this generation of North-Eastern greats there has been one common cry: "Away the Lads ... anywhere but Newcastle."

Here SHOOT reveals the Newcastle team that might have been – but somehow, sooner or later, they all slipped through the net.

Together they could have taken on anyone. Newcastle United fans, who haven't seen a major trophy since Bobby Moncur lifted the old European Fairs Cup 20 years ago, must constantly ask themselves why it never happened.

Practically the only home-grown success currently at St James' Park is defender Kenny Wharton.

Chris Waddle, Kevin Richardson and Neil Aspin explain the reasons why so many have rejected a future at Newcastle – and offer a glimmer of hope for an end to the Geordie torture.

*Kevin Richardson:* 'The Newcastle scouting staff wanted to sign me when I was a youngster.

But the facilities for bringing in the young lads just weren't good enough.

The weight training was inadequate and the general feeling was that everything was geared for the professionals and not the apprentices.

They didn't seem to care much about the young players. At Everton, at least I felt wanted for a start.

There were big indoor training facilities with plenty of weights – and although it was hard work, it was also enjoyable.

Now, of course, there is a different staff at St James' Park with different ideas and I hope things have changed.'

*Neil Aspin:* 'There is a vicious circle at Newcastle. While success breeds success at many other clubs, Newcastle haven't won anything for two decades.

Players such as Paul Gascoigne, Peter Beardsley and Chris Waddle would no doubt have stayed if the club had been more ambitious.

Now the kids in the city support other clubs like Liverpool because that way they think they might have a chance of celebrating success.

I grew up supporting Leeds because they had won things and that's why I went straight to Elland Road when I had the chance.'

*Chris Waddle:* 'Maybe Newcastle United just don't think big enough. They used to make star signings in the old days, but now it just doesn't seem to happen.

But the youth system at St James' park is much better nowadays and Gazza is living proof of that. He has come through the ranks. There are one or two others waiting for their chance.

Perhaps Newcastle let their players go too easily, but then there is a general lack of ambition. It's hard to keep players at a club that doesn't win anything.'

# ANFIELD'S

## Many players often spend years in the reserves before getting a first team chance at Liverpool

**F**ORCING your way into the Anfield first team is harder than breaking into Buckingham Palace – as many ex-Liverpool reserve team players will tell you.

Numerous players, both seasoned pros and aspiring apprentices, have been left lanquishing in Anfield's twilight zone because of Liverpool's enormous squad.

"I joined them at 16 and went on to score 50 or 60 goals in the reserves but still couldn't break into the first team," says striker Tommy Tynan, now banging them in for Plymouth.

"I enjoyed it there, but with players like Phil Boersma, Steve Heighway and David Fairclough unable to gain a regular first team place what chance did I have?

"There were even eight or nine experienced professionals in the 'A' team – Liverpool's third side."

Steve Ogrizovic spent four years in the Anfield wilderness.

"I was Ray Clemence's understudy and my only real chance to get a go was when he was injured, which wasn't often," says the Coventry goalkeeper.

"I played just four games and now realise I stayed there two years too long. But you are taught by the best people in the country and the experience has kept me in good stead since."

Many other players have failed in their bid for Anfield glory. Everton's Kevin Sheedy, Dave Watson and Alan Harper, Paul Jewell (now at Wigan), Blackburn's Howard Gayle and Hull's Ken De Mange, who partners Sheedy and Liverpool's Ronnie Whelan, one of the successful few, in the Republic of Ireland midfield.

Big money buys often find it just as tough. Players like Ray Kennedy and Terry McDermott took seasons to establish themselves. Others like Frank McGarvey never made the grade and left.

Paul Walsh was one of the most recent players to find life too tough at Anfield.

He arrived as an England international and established striker with Charlton and Luton. But having struggled to gain a place, he lost it through injury and never regained it.

Before his £500,000 transfer to Spurs

*Howard Gayle.*

*Steve Staunton.*

in February 1988, he partnered players like Jan Molby, Kevin Macdonald, Gary Ablett and super kid Wayne Harrison – who never made his first team debut.

But Walsh's plight in the Anfield reserves was nothing compared to that of Brian Kettle. Walsh had had enough after nearly four years with the Reds, but Kettle stuck to it for twice as long, despite winning more reserve Championship medals than he made first team appearances.

# WAITING GAME

Coventry 'keeper Steve Ogrizovic spent four years in the Liverpool wilderness.

Kettle was unfortunate to be Phil Neal's understudy. Neal set a club record of 417 consecutive appearances, Kettle made just six.

A boyhood fan, Kettle, who joined Liverpool in May 1973 and left more than seven years later, says: "We were watched by an average gate of more than 1,200 in the reserves. It's as big as some Fourth Division sides but it doesn't compare to the first team.

"I remember once we needed just a point against Wolves to win the Central League title and 3,000 fans turned out. In all I won seven Central League Championship medals."

The Liverpool management rejected offers for Kettle of around £75,000 from clubs like Swansea, then a first Division side, Stoke and Blackburn.

"I didn't desperately want to leave and they wouldn't let me go as long as they were playing in Europe."

Kettle eventually joined Wigan for £30,000 in 1980 and is now manager of non-League South Liverpool. He helps run the community programme back at Anfield, so his ties with the club still remain strong.

"My time under Bill Shankly and Bob Paisley has stood me well as a manager," adds Kettle, who now aims to achieve as a boss the success and recognition that eluded him as a player at Liverpool.

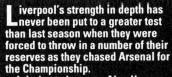

Paul Walsh.

Liverpool's strength in depth has never been put to a greater test than last season when they were forced to throw in a number of their reserves as they chased Arsenal for the Championship.

Injuries to key men Alan Hansen, Jim Beglin, Bruce Grobbelaar and Gary Gillespie left gaping holes in their defence and manager Kenny Dalglish called Steve Staunton, Alex Watson and Barry Venison in from the cold to help quell the crisis.

The 20-year-old Staunton proved a revelation in the left-back spot, going on to win international honours with the Republic of Ireland. Watson, brother of Dave at Everton, proved a more than adequate cover in the heart of The Reds defence and Venison covered admirably at right-back when Steve Nicol was moved in to the middle of the back four.

And 'keeper Mike Hooper proved an outstanding success in place of meningitis victim Grobbelaar.

Indeed such is Liverpool's depth of talent now that they could field two sides that would be among the contenders for honours in the First Division.

# SOCCER'S GOLDEN GIRLS

**T**ake heart, Bobby Robson! England's women's team were proud winners of the 'Mundialito' or mini World Cup, held in Italy last year.

On their road to the Final they played the likes of France and beat a very athletic team from the United States in the Semi-Final.

The Final against Italy was a classic. England had been leading through Linda Curl, the tournament's top scorer, right up until the last minutes of normal time, but then conceded a goal just when victory was so near at hand.

"It was a psychological battle as much as a physical one to muster renewed strength for extra-time," remembers Curl.

While our ladies have few troubles on the field, off the pitch they have to fight hard for recognition. The secretary of the Women's Football Association, Linda Whitehead, explains: "We are very much the poor relations."

Million pound transfers are almost commonplace in the men's game and many top stars make enough during their playing careers to retire on.

In contrast, the women's game is completely

*England stars Kerry Davis (top), Marianne Spacey (centre) and Liz Deighan (dark shirt below).*

amateur with only expenses paid and sponsorship minimal.

But the ladies' game in some other European countries receives better support, particularly in Italy and Scandinavia. Some English internationals have gone to seek their fortunes in the professional Italian Ladies' League.

Kerry Davis has played at several clubs there, learnt the language and is doing very well; and Debbie Bampton, England's captain, was there for a year. But even in Italy their earnings, which are not always regular, are dwarfed by those of their male counterparts.

Marianne Spacey laments: "It's a vicious circle. The media say they don't cover our matches because there is not enough interest but the interest will not be generated if we don't get the coverage in the first place."

All the women players are convinced that if people did come to their matches they would be impressed by the quality of skill.

## Attractive

Marianne Spacey believes that the woman's game is more attractive to watch: "It is more uninhibited and free flowing and not riddled with offside."

Linda Curl adds that while the men's game is "faster and more physical" this is not to suggest there is anything "cissy" about the women's football.

"I often come off the pitch with some fairly heavy bruises, but I don't think there is the cynical element you can get in the men's game."

There are signs that the women are beginning to win recognition for their talents. The national team's kit is provided by Spall Sportswear and the W.F.A. has a sponsorship deal with Niagara Therapy.

Better still, Channel 4 showed highlights of the W.F.A Cup Final played on April 22 between Leasowe from Liverpool and Friends of Fulham.

International stars such as Spacey, who plays for Fulham, saw this as their big chance to promote the women's game in front of a national audience.

Many of the watching millions were surprised at the high skills shown in the game which Leasowe won 3-2.

● For further details of women's football, write to the Women's FA at 448/450 Hanging Ditch, The Corn Exchange, Manchester M4 3ES.

# ALAN McINALLY

## Bayern Munich

Dustman, baker,
electrician, jungle-
fighter. How some of today's
leading players began their
working lives.

# JUST

As a part-timer with Winsford, Neville Southall combined football with his duties as a cook.

**F**ifty years and more ago, many a promising footballer, leaving school and dreaming of a career in the game, stepped on the first hopeful rung of the ladder to fame by joining the groundstaff of a League club.

After the war, in the early 1950's came youth schemes, with Chelsea and Manchester United the pioneers. The purpose was twofold: clubs could nurture their own juniors in quantity, and home-produced talent would be a satisfying answer to escalating transfer fees.

Across the country, other clubs rapidly followed suit. Apprentices became the next category, and schoolboys could be registered with League clubs for training.

Now the description "apprentices" has given way to "trainees" for talented boys of 16 and 17 eager to break into the game on leaving school.

The Government's Youth Training Scheme provides another inroad but, more and more, the search for stars is taking big clubs into non-League football, with spectacular success.

Many of today's big names began their working lives doing other jobs and playing football part-time, or just for fun.

**Chris Waddle**, for instance. As a teenager employed in a sausage-seasoning factory up in the North-East, and playing on Saturday afternoons for tiny Tow Law Town.

Then Newcastle United took him on, and after over four seasons of first-team football at St James's Park, he moved to London for fame and fortune with Tottenham.

**Bruce Grobbelaar** was a jungle-fighting corporal in the Rhodesian Army before coming to England in search of a career in football – first with Crewe Alexandra and, ultimately, helping Liverpool pile up the honours as one of the game's finest goalkeepers.

In Scotland, outside the top-bracket clubs, most footballers are part-time. So, when Nottingham Forest signed defender **Martin Clark** from Clyde for £100,000 last February, he had to work out his notice as a hospital porter in Glasgow's Western Infirmary before actually joining them.

Still with Forest, left-back **Stuart Pearce**, who captained them to three Cup Finals last season, began his

# THE JOB!

*Chris Waddle*

football next door to Wembley with non-League Wealdstone. His "proper" job, before Coventry City launched him into First Division orbit, was . . . electrician.

After the 1988 FA Cup Final, another Wealdstone product climbed Wembley's famous steps to receive a winner's medal from Princess Diana in the hand that used to carry a building-site hod. He was Wimbledon's **Vinny Jones**.

Last November, 19-year-old **Giuliano Mairorana** was working in an Italian menswear shop in Cambridge – except for Saturday afternoons, spent playing for Histon, in the Eastern Counties League.

Manchester United manager Alex Ferguson heard a whisper . . . invited Giuliano to play for them as a guest in a testimonial at Birmingham.

Next day, he joined United in a £30,000 transfer . . . and four months later Maiorana's left-wing skill was dazzling not only Arsenal, but millions of Sunday viewers of The Match on ITV.

**Dale Gordon** was among the stars of Norwich City's out standing season in 1988-89. But did you know that before becoming a professional at Carrow Road he was selling T-shirts from a stall on Great Yarmouth sea-front?

Dynamic 5ft 5in midfield player **Mark Ward** was a £250,000 snip for West Ham in the summer of 1985. Good business for Oldham who, two years earlier, had signed him for just £10,000 from non-League Northwich Victoria. Before turning to full-time football, Mark worked in a bakery.

**Graham Roberts**, now 30, has won honours galore with England (six caps), Tottenham, Rangers and Chelsea, whom he captained back to the First Division last season. He has never forgotten, though, that while playing for non-League Weymouth before he came

into big-time football with Spurs he was working as a fitter's mate at Southampton Docks.

**Joe McLaughlin**, another of Chelsea's 1989 promotion stars, was a qualified plumber back home in Scotland while playing for Morton.

As we said, part-time players outnumber the full-timers in Scotland.

But striker **Frank McAvennie** beats the lot. He had 15 jobs in Glasgow before he became a footballer. They included roadsweeper, motor mechanic, painter and decorator, waiter, labourer and van-boy.

Frank kept Saturdays clear, though, to play junior football for Johnstone Burgh. That's where he was spotted by St Mirren manager Jim Clunie . . . and sharpshooter McAvennie was on his way to stardom – to West Ham after four seasons with St Mirren, then to Celtic and, with five Scotland caps to his name, back to London and West Ham last season.

*Don McVicar*

**Don McVicar**, St Johnstone captain and full-back, was entitled to be a tired man at the end of last season's Scottish Cup Semi-Final at Parkhead.

While Rangers' stars were still snoozing in five-star hotel luxury, he was up as usual at 4.30 on Semi-Final morning and on his way to work as the village postie in Monifieth.

Liverpool-born **Andy Mutch**, "other half" of the formidable strike partnership – with Steve Bull – that rocketed Wolves from Fourth Division to Second in the last two seasons, used to sell fridges for a living.

That was when he played part-time with non-League Southport, who sold him to Wolves for £5,000 in 1986.

Ten years ago, playing for part-timers Winsford, was a goalkeeper who, away from football, had done such varied jobs as dustman, cook and building worker.

Eventually, he got his League chance with Bury. Today he is among the world's top 'keepers. The name is **Neville Southall**, of Everton and Wales.

**John Aldridge** was once a sheet-metal worker on an assembly line. Big money and Championship medals with Liverpool, International caps for the Republic of Ireland could not have been further from his mind as he played part-time on Merseyside for **South** Liverpool.

But the pal working alongside him at British Leyland was the brother of Len Ashurst, then manager of Newport County, and tipped him off that Aldridge was "a bit of a player."

So at 20, John gave up the "day job" and move to South Wales to become a professional footballer. Eleven years later, via five seasons at Somerton Park and three with Oxford United, he was at his scoring peak with Liverpool . . . at the time Newport County folded.

Norwich City's **Andy Townsend** was a major force behind the club's success last season but when he first received a phone call offering him a shot at the big time he thought it was a joke.

He explains: "I was sitting in the office one day when the phone rang and the voice said, 'Hello, this is Lawrie McMenemy speaking.' I thought it was one of the lads in the office having a laugh but sure enough it was him."

At the time Andy was playing non-League football for Weymouth and working as a computer operator for the London Borough of Greenwich.

He says: "It was shift work at the council so on match days I would have to start the 7.00am shift then rush to Waterloo to catch the train down to Weymouth.

"Unfortunately, the last train back to London is a slow one so after evening matches I didn't arrive back until three in the morning. Then I was up again at half-past-six to go to work. It was hard at times but I enjoyed it."

*Andy Townsend*

# BONNER THE BRAVE

**C**ELTIC and Republic of Ireland goalkeeper Pat Bonner, could well have been grabbing headlines as a striker.

But Pat's dream of becoming a top scorer faded when as a 12-year-old severe pains in his side, triggered off by the running demanded of him during a game, forced the youngster to drop any idea of playing in an outfield position.

"I decided to have a go at keeping goal," reveals Bonner, "because like most Irish kids I played both soccer and Gaelic football. As a matter of fact, the Gaelic game is more popular in Eire than soccer.

"It's a sport that features plenty of kicking and catching the ball, and a fair amount of bodily contact, so, in that respect, switching to goalkeeper seemed a sensible move."

Eventually Pat's abdominal pains were diagnosed as a hernia, which was successfully treated on the operating table.

Even a return to full fitness failed to rekindle Pat's ambition to become a shooting star.

"I've always loved the Gaelic game, and was good enough at it to play at senior level until I was 17, when I dropped out to really concentrate on a future between the posts," he says.

"Playing Gaelic football in midfield, as I did, was an education! Believe me, I learned all about flying boots, careless fists, and hard, jabbing elbows.

## Tough guys

"I was a kid competing with grown men, and I revelled in it!

"All the running, catching and kicking, on and off the ball, toughened me up. Dodging the straying boots, fists, and spiteful elbows, did wonders for my fitness!

"Seriously though, I have a lot to thank Gaelic football for. It improved my handling, my timing, my awareness of what was going on around me, and it certainly taught me how to look after myself in a crowded goal-mouth!

"If I hadn't made it as a goalkeeper, I'd have been delighted to continue playing the Gaelic game in my native Donegal."

Pat's first step to soccer stardom came shortly after his 18th birthday when the late Jock Stein, then manager of Celtic, signed him from a local team called Keadue Rovers.

Pat, a first team regular since the 1980-81 season, suffered a set-back six years later when a back injury put his future in doubt.

"For most of the 1987-88 Championship winning season I was in some pain from a disc pressing on a nerve in my back," Pat recalls.

"It started to get worse during the European Championship games, and the doctors decided to remove that part of the disc."

Despite the signings of Ian Andrews and Alan Rough for the start of last season, Pat battled back to recapture his first team spot at Parkhead.

"Their arrival gave me the ideal opportunity of ensuring I made a full recovery to match fitness," he says.

The courage and strength gained on the Gaelic football field had stood brave Bonner in good stead.

West Ham veteran Liam Brady prepares to volley a shot in front of Sheffield Wednesday striker Gary Bannister.

# HEARTS

John Robertson's rapid return to Hearts gave him more than a new lease of life.

It also provided JR with the chance to shoot himself into the record books as the most successful Tynecastle marksman of all time.

It was in the summer of 1988 that the stocky striker decided against a new contract with the Edinburgh outfit and plumped instead for a £750,000 move across the border to Newcastle United.

But the 25-year-old goal ace struggled to repeat his Tynecastle scoring form for the Geordie giants and failed to capture a regular first team slot.

The relegation alarm bells were already ringing when QPR manager Jim Smith was lured to St. James' Park to trigger off a mass clearout.

Hearts stepped in to provide the perfect answer to Robertson's dilemma when they took him back to Edinburgh by returning the cash they'd received for him less than six months earlier.

He returned to a hero's welcome,

# WARMER

## Robbo aims to beat goal target

Manager Alex McDonald (above).
Joe Colquhoun finds the going tough against Morton.

helping Hearts to a tremendous home victory over Rangers, and it wasn't long before he was back on the goal trail.

Even a stomach muscle injury sustained months earlier, and which certainly didn't help his efforts at Newcastle, could not keep him down.

Robertson pushed himself through the pain barrier and received sympathetic support from Tynecastle boss Alex McDonald.

"The boss was brilliant," acknowledges the Edinburgh-born striker. "He knew I couldn't train properly and that I was only half-fit but he never gave up on me.

"He used me as substitute and the move worked well. I grabbed a few goals and suddenly people were telling me I was well up the club's all-time scoring list."

### Lethal JR

Robertson's late winner in the final derby clash of the 1988-89 campaign was his 150th for Hearts – and underlined his liking for finding the net against city rival Hibs, victims of JR's lethal finishing on many previous occasions.

"The goal was memorable because it was my first one at Tynecastle since rejoining the club from Newcastle and for it to settle an Edinburgh derby was a super bonus," he said.

Now he has his sights set on the legendary trio of Alfie Conn, Willie Bauld and Jimmy Wardhaugh, who inspired Hearts to success in all three domestic competitions during the 1950s and still hold the top three places in the club's goal chart.

Wardhaugh leads the way with the 206 he scored in all competitions between 1949 and 1956 and Robertson admits: "I'd love to beat his record.

"With a bit of luck I could create a

new record in a couple of years, although my main aim is simply to make sure Hearts are in there fighting for the major honours again.

"When I went to Newcastle I was desperate to prove myself in the English First Division and I had high hopes for myself and the club. But things didn't work out.

"The chance to return to Tynecastle was too good to miss. In some ways it was as if I'd never been away and, of course, I had no problems settling in."

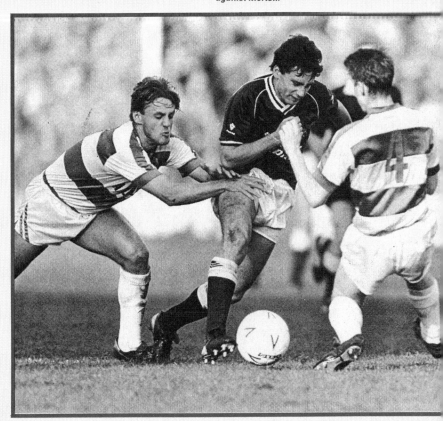

67

## GORDON COWANS

Gordon Cowans might not have enjoyed the best of luck since returning to Aston Villa from Italy but in his daughter's eyes the elegant midfielder will always be a winner.

## VINNY JONES

Vinny Jones is used to shooting down his rivals but the Leeds hard man loves nothing better than a stroll in the countryside, a spot of fishing and the chance to try out his shotgun on his father's land.

## PAUL ELLIOTT

Paul Elliott's lifestyle was a bit different. The England Under-21 star was at home in the lovely city of Pisa when we visited him last year enjoying an ice cream in front of the famous leaning tower. It's hard for some!

### RICKY HILL

It's hats off to Ricky Hill, the nightclub loving former England star. The skilful midfielder was as quick to welcome us into his home as he was at going past the despairing tackles of his opponents.

### MARK WALTERS

We took a trip up to Scotland last Christmas to meet the new Rangers hero Mark Walters. The wing wizard was quiet and polite but obviously prefers to let his feet do the talking on the pitch. Something his Premier Division opponents will vouch he does very well.

### CHRIS MORRIS

Have you heard the one about the Cornishman who has played League football in England and Scotland and represented the Republic of Ireland at international level? Meet Chris Morris who loves to tinkle the keys on his piano and is also a chiropodist.

**1** Brian McClair carried a massive £2 million price tag when Manchester United manager Alex Ferguson asked Celtic if they were prepared to sell their ace goalscorer. Fergie's smooth talking worked wonders. United snapped him up for a mere £850,000.

**2** Bob Bishop, Manchester United's chief scout in Belfast, saw a 15-year-old destroy his boys' team. He rang Matt Busby, Manchester United's manager at the time, to say: "Matt, I

*George Best*

*Brian McClair*

think I've found a genius." "Who is that?" enquired Busby. "A lad named George Best," replied Bishop.

**3** Duncan Edwards, who died at the age of 21 as a result of injuries received in the Munich air crash, made his League debut for United against Cardiff in April 1953 at the age of 16. At the age of 18 years and 183 days, he became the youngest player to wear a full England shirt. When he died, he had already made 18 England appearances.

**4** Spring-heeled Denis Law, known as 'The King' in his Old Trafford days, developed his incredible heading skills by heading a paper ball, tethered to a clothes rack in the kitchen of his parents' home.

**5** Manchester United's famous red and white banners were draped with black after the Munich air crash. The combination of red, white and black later became the club's official colours.

**6** Bryan Robson's transfer from West Bromwich Albion for £1.8 million in the 1981-82 season shattered the transfer record between British clubs. Announcing the signing, manager Ron Atkinson said: "He is the most complete midfield player in the game. He can defend, he can create and he can inspire all around him." Big Ron forgot to say Bryan could also score goals!

**7** Tommy Docherty was sacked by United in July 1977 after announcing he was leaving his wife, Agnes, to live with the wife of the club's physiotherapist. The Doc said: "I have been punished for falling in love. What I have done has nothing to do with my track record as manager."

**8** Horror of horrors … United played at Maine Road after the Second World

*Bryan Robson*

# KNOW ABOUT UNITED

*Bobby Charlton*

up the famous 39 steps to the Royal Box, and in his moment of triumph he had forgotten to remove it. "I have wanted to apologise ever since," says Bryan.

**12** Don Revie, Jock Stein, Malcolm Allison and Brian Clough were all considered as possible replacements for Matt Busby when he retired as manager of United. Wilf McGuinness, promoted from the ranks, beat them all to the job in June 1969.

**13** Tommy Taylor carried a pair of football boots stuffed in his jacket pocket when he travelled from Barnsley to sign for the 'Busby Babes' in a £29,999 deal. The transfer price was fixed at £1 short of £30,000 to protect Tommy from the pressure of being the first £30,000 player.

**14** Alex Ferguson told radio listeners that United were laying a carpet of artificial turf at Old Trafford. "What colour?" enquired the interviewer. "Uh, red of course," replied Alex. Only the sharpest listeners realised that the interview was being conducted on 1st April, 1988.

**15** United rebel George Best missed a week's training in January 1972. He was promptly dropped, fined, and ordered to leave his new house at Bramhall and take 'digs' where his lifestyle could be supervised.

War. Manchester City, United's deadly rivals, kindly lent United the use of their ground when Old Trafford was badly blitzed by bombs. United played on City's ground till the start of the 1949-50 season when they moved back to bright, new stands at Old Trafford.

**9** The 1979 FA Cup Final between Manchester United and Arsenal became known as the 'five minute Final'. Two-nil down with five minutes left, United hit back with goals from Gordon McQueen and Sammy McIlroy. But seconds from the end, Alan Sunderland scored Arsenal's winner.

**10** Manchester United splashed out £900,000 to sign Frank Stapleton, Arsenal's Republic of Ireland striker. Yet they could have had him for nothing! Frank was invited to train with United at the age of 15. He attended a summer coaching camp, but the United coaches failed to recognise his talents … and Arsenal moved in.

**11** Bryan Robson is still haunted by the day he broke Wembley protocol by wearing a hat when he received the FA Cup from a member of the Royal Family. United had beaten Brighton in 1983, but when the Princess handed Bryan the Cup, he was wearing a silk hat. A United supporter planted the cap on his head when he marched

*Mark Hughes*

**16** The museum at Old Trafford contains a replica of the European Cup United won by beating Benfica in 1968. The trophy has cost more than £10,000 to make.

**17** Football writers reached for their record books at the start of the 1985-86 season. United stormed to the top of the First Division with 10 straight wins. One more would equal Spurs' record, but United could only draw at Luton. They suffered their first League defeat on November 9, against Sheffield Wednesday, and won only seven times in their next 23 games.

**18** Mark Hughes scored 25 goals in 55 games in 1984-85, his first full season. Mark was voted the Professional Footballers' Association's Young Player of the Year.

**19** Bobby Charlton, who played 106 times for England, wore the Manchester United shirt on 606 occasions. He represented his country at all levels – England Schoolboys, Youth, Under-23 and at full international status. He scored 49 goals for England.

**20** Craziest transfer deal ever … United persuaded Stockport to part with Hughie McLenahan in 1927 in exchange for three freezers of ice cream.

LIVERPOOL'S success at home and abroad over the last 25 glorious years is unrivalled virtually throughout Europe ... and possibly the world.

Since the memorable Shankly era the club has gone from strength to strength and only the unfortunate UEFA ban has prevented them from adding more European honours to those they continue to collect with impeccable consistency on the domestic front.

In 25 years the Mighty Reds have registered no fewer than 12 League Championship success and the lowest they have ever finished in the First Division is seventh!

# LIVE 25 YEARS O

In fact since 1973 they have finished a season outside the top two on just one occasion – in 1981 when they managed a humble fifth place.

Liverpool, who have never played outside the top two divisions since they were formed in 1893, have also proved themselves to be masterful in the cut and thrust world of Cup competition.

They won the FA Cup for the first time in the club's history in 1965 and have now lifted the coveted trophy a

further three times ... in 1974, 1986 and 1989.

For four seasons – between 1981 and 1984 – they also dominated the League Cup competition.

And, until the Heysel tragedy of 1985, Liverpool were also masters of European competition, on course to rival the achievements of the legendary Real Madrid side of the 1950s.

They reached the final of the European Cup Winners' Cup in 1966, losing by the odd goal to Borussia

Dortmund after extra time, and served notice of their European intentions by lifting the UEFA Cup in 1973 and 1976.

It was in 1977 that Liverpool truly arrived on the European scene when they beat Borussia Moenchengladbach with a classic performance to lift the Champions Cup, a feat they were to repeat a year later against Bruges at Wembley.

Three years on they were again undisputed Champions of Europe as Alan Kennedy scored the only goal of

Left: Liverpool celebrate their FA Cup victory over Everton in 1986 that clinched the double. Above: Alan Kennedy scores the Reds' winner against Real Madrid in the 1981 European Cup Final.

## Liverpool honours since 1964

**FA Cup winners:** 1965, 1974, 1986, 1989.
**FA Cup runners-up:** 1971, 1977, 1988.
**League Cup winners:** 1981, 1982, 1983, 1984.
**League Cup runners-up:** 1978, 1987.
**League Super Cup winners:** 1986.
**European Cup winners:** 1977, 1978, 1981, 1984.
**European Cup runners-up:** 1985.
**European Cup-Winners' Cup runners-up:** 1966.
**UEFA Cup winners:** 1973, 1976.
**European Super Cup winners:** 1977.
**World Club Championship runners-up:** 1981.

### Liverpool's League positions over the past 25 years

| | | | |
|---|---|---|---|
| 1963-64: | 1st | 1976-77: | 1st |
| 1964-65: | 7th | 1977-78: | 2nd |
| 1965-66: | 1st | 1978-79: | 1st |
| 1966-67: | 5th | 1979-80: | 1st |
| 1967-68: | 3rd | 1980-81: | 5th |
| 1968-69: | 2nd | 1981-82: | 1st |
| 1969-70: | 5th | 1982-83: | 1st |
| 1970-71: | 5th | 1983-84: | 1st |
| 1971-72: | 3rd | 1984-85: | 2nd |
| 1972-73: | 1st | 1985-86: | 1st |
| 1973-74: | 2nd | 1986-87: | 2nd |
| 1974-75: | 2nd | 1987-88: | 1st |
| 1975-76: | 1st | 1988-89: | 2nd |

the Paris final against none other than Real Madrid.

When they beat Roma 'in their own backyard' after a penalty shoot-out in 1984 they were on the brink of immortality. Sadly the events of Heysel the following year halted their march.

Last season the Hillsborough disaster threatened to do likewise on the domestic scene but, with the type of professionalism unique to the mighty Merseysiders, they recovered their composure in time to win the FA Cup and come within 90 seconds of doing the double.

In terms of achievements on the field the last 25 years have been truly glorious for Liverpool Football Club.

# BOSS FUN

"I want our striker to show more aggression up front. Tell him his horse has just lost at Kempton."

"Before you settle in, boss, the chairman has asked me to inform you that you've been sacked"

"I had this new strip designed especially for you"

"The press have given you a cracking write-up, boss ... compared you with Bobby Robson"

"They're twice as fit since I introduced the punch-bag, boss"

"Instead of a raise – I'm going to give you a £2,000 bonus for every goal you score."

"When you sold me that player for £500,000 you forgot to tell me he has to leave the pitch every ten minutes to go to the loo"

"Our manager is so used to praying for miracles he should have been a vicar"

Mark Bright

# High flying Eagles

Ian Wright

**T**HE sharpshooting bravado of strikers Mark Bright and Ian Wright may set Crystal Palace pulses racing, but at Selhurst Park nobody dares mention the dawn of a new era.

The last time the Eagles were tipped for greatness, Palace, the so-called "Team of the 80's", nearly went out of business!

Boardroom strife and a managerial merry-go-round, which left supporters dizzy, sapped the confidence and belief of a young team whose exciting brand of football won the 1977 and 1978 FA Youth Cups.

By the time chairman Ron Noades took up the Selhurst reins in January 1981, Palace had lost promising manager Terry Venables to Queens Park Rangers and were bottom of the First Division. The club was on the verge of bankruptcy and it needed a miracle to save them from relegation.

The side that Dario Gradi – Palace's fourth manager in a whirlwind three-month period – took down to Division Two in 1981 bore scant resemblance to the swashbuckling team of youngsters that Venables had steered to the Second Division Championship only two years before.

A record crowd of 51,482 (thousands more were locked outside) had squeezed into Selhurst Park on a balmy Friday evening in May to watch Palace beat Burnley 2-0 and confirm their return to the First Division after a six-year absence.

Teenagers like Peter Nicholas, Terry Fenwick, Vince Hilaire, Ian Walsh, Billy Gilbert, Jerry Murphy and Kenny Sansom had the footballing world at their feet.

The myth was that, under Venables' continued guidance, they would make Palace a major force in English football. Reality proved much harder.

Welsh International Nicholas, who won his second Division Two Championship medal, exactly ten years after his first, when Chelsea won promotion last season, believes the Palace kids became a victim of their own success.

Palace started well enough in Division One – they led the table after a crushing 4-1 win against an Ipswich Town side sprinkled with Internationals in late September – but Nicholas says they could not handle defeat.

One particular defeat, in December 1979, underlined just how much Palace had to learn. Not surprisingly it came at Anfield, home of the reigning Champions Liverpool.

Terry Venables' exciting youngsters arrived on Merseyside third in Division One.

## Slipped

After losing 3-0, Palace won just five of their 25 remaining games that season. They slipped down the table and finished a disappointing 13th.

That decline became a crisis the following season. Palace lost nine of their opening ten League games. And in October they suffered a loss from which they failed to recover – Venables' departure to QPR.

"Terry's going marked the end of the "team of the 80's," says Nicholas, now approaching his 30th birthday.

"Terry moved when the board refused to give him money with which to improve the squad. The directors' reasoning became clear when they sold the club to Ron Noades three months later."

Nicholas then played under three managers – Ernie Walley, Malcolm Allison and Dario Gradi – in as many months while Palace became embedded at the foot of Division One. He jumped at the chance to join Arsenal for £400,000 in March 1981.

Such disillusionment spread through the Palace team, whose haul of only 19 points is one of the worst in First Division history.

There had been no dramatic improvement when Nicholas returned to play another 50 games for Palace three seasons later.

Nicholas recalls they were still struggling. Steve Kember had been hired and fired as manager in his absence and Alan Mullery – the club's sixth manager in less than two years – re-signed Nicholas.

## Improve

"The team managed to avoid relegation to Division Three and things started to improve after another managerial change in 1984 when Steve Coppell joined the club," says the Newport-born player, who joined Luton Town in January 1985.

"I don't regret my time at Palace at all," says Nicholas. "We learnt a great deal about success and failure very early in our careers. That experience stood us in good stead."

It certainly helped Sansom, whose 86 International appearances has made him England's most-capped full-back. And it helped Fenwick, who played for England in the 1986 World Cup Finals.

Tricky winger Vince Hilaire, by far the most skilful player to emerge, did not quite fulfil his potential, although he is still tormenting Second Division defences with Leeds.

Palace fans now have a new hero in Ian Wright. And his lethal partnership with Mark Bright has helped make the Selhurst Park Eagle fly confidently again. After a decade of heartache, Palace are looking ahead to a Wright Bright future.

GOA

# LDEN BULL

## Wolves' prolific striker keeps banging 'em in!

Molineux scoring machine Steve Bull last season became the first player since the War to hit 100 goals in just two terms ... and here's how the wonder of Wolves did it.

### 1987-88

| | |
|---|---|
| Aug 15 **v Scarborough** | 1 |
| Aug 25 **v Notts County (Littlewoods)** | 2 |
| Aug 29 **v Hereford** | 1 |
| Aug 31 **v Scunthorpe** | 2 |
| Sep 5 **v Cardiff** | 1 |
| Sep 12 **v Crewe** | 1 |
| Sep 16 **v Peterborough** | 1 |
| Sep 22 **v Man. City (Littlewoods)** | 1 |
| Sep 26 **v Torquay** | 1 |
| Sep 29 **v Rochdale** | 1 |
| Oct 10 **v Carlisle** | 1 |
| Oct 17 **v Tranmere** | 1 |
| Oct 20 **v Cambridge** | 1 |
| Oct 26 **v Swansea (Sherpa Van)** | 1 |
| Nov 3 **v Swansea** | 1 |
| Nov 14 **v Cheltenham (FA Cup)** | 3 |
| Nov 24 **v Bristol City (Sherpa Van)** | 2 |
| Dec 19 **v Orient** | 2 |
| Jan 1 **v Hereford** | 2 |
| Jan 19 **v Brentford (Sherpa Van)** | 3 |
| Feb 6 **v Cardiff** | 1 |
| Feb 9 **v Peterborough (Sherpa Van)** | 2 |
| Feb 13 **v Exeter** | 3 |
| Feb 27 **v Bolton** | 2 |
| March 8 **v Torquay (Sherpa Van)** | 1 |
| March 26 **v Darlington** | 3 |
| April 2 **v Burnley** | 1 |
| April 4 **v Colchester** | 2 |
| April 12 **v Notts County (Sherpa Van)** | 1 |
| April 19 **v Notts County (Sherpa Van)** | 2 |
| April 23 **v Swansea** | 1 |
| April 26 **v Newport** | 2 |
| May 2 **v Hartlepool** | 2 |
| **TOTAL 52** | |

### 1988-89

| | |
|---|---|
| Aug 30 **v Birmingham (Littlewoods)** | 2 |
| Sep 20 **v Aldershot** | 1 |
| Sep 25 **v Swansea** | 2 |
| Oct 1 **Port Vale** | 2 |
| Oct 15 **v Wigan** | 1 |
| Oct 22 **v Bolton** | 1 |
| Oct 29 **v Gillingham** | 1 |
| Nov 5 **v Southend** | 1 |
| Nov 12 **v Huddersfield** | 2 |
| Nov 26 **v Preston** | 4 |
| Nov 30 **v Hereford (Sherpa Van)** | 1 |
| Dec 13 **v Port Vale (Sherpa Van)** | 4 |
| Dec 17 **v Mansfield** | 3 |
| Dec 31 **v Brentford** | 1 |
| Jan 2 **v Chester** | 1 |
| Jan 10 **v Cardiff** | 1 |
| Jan 24 **v Bristol City (Sherpa Van)** | 3 |
| Feb 11 **v Fulham** | 3 |
| Feb 28 **v Blackpool** | 1 |
| Mar 4 **v Bolton** | 1 |
| Mar 14 **v Gillingham** | 1 |
| Mar 18 **v Bury** | 3 |
| Mar 22 **v Hereford (Sherpa Van)** | 1 |
| April 1 **v Mansfield** | 1 |
| April 8 **v Brentford** | 1 |
| April 12 **v Torquay (Sherpa Van)** | 2 |
| April 15 **v Aldershot** | 1 |
| April 29 **v Bristol City** | 2 |
| May 6 **v Northampton** | 1 |
| May 9 **v Sheffield Utd** | 1 |
| **TOTAL 50** | |

*Aldershot's Darren Anderson witnesses the charging Bull in action.*

# VINTAGE

ONE ... Gary shows his predatory instincts as he turns and fires a shot towards the Northern Ireland goal during a European Championship qualifying match in 1986 ...
TWO ... The net bulges and England are on their way to a 3-0 Wembley win ...
THREE ... Gary and Terry Butcher turn away in delight to celebrate one of his two goals on another memorable international night.

**1**

**2**

**3**

# LINEKER

## THE GOALS THAT MADE GARY GREAT

Eire's Mick McCarthy and 'keeper Pat Bonner are powerless to resist as Gary clocks up his first England goal in a 2-1 win at Wembley in 1985.

England's Gary Lineker has endured the sort of barren run in front of goal that would have had most strikers pulling their hair out in frustration and anger.

But despite hitting the leanest spell of his international career Lineker insists he's never lost the confidence and ability which earned him nationwide acclaim and a king's ransom to join Barcelona after the 1986 World Cup Finals.

After an abysmal time during the European Championship Finals in 1988 and subsequent illness, however, many believe he is not the same player which once terrorised defences the world over.

For those who doubt he will ever recapture the form which made him the golden boy of English soccer not too long ago here's a pictorial reminder of some of the international goals which shot him to fame…

Gary celebrates the first of his life-saving three goals in the 3-0 win over Poland during the 1986 World Cup Finals. he ended the tournament as the leading scorer with six goals.

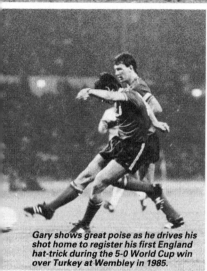

Gary shows great poise as he drives his shot home to register his first England hat-trick during the 5-0 World Cup win over Turkey at Wembley in 1985.

Gary destroyed Spain virtually single-handed with all four goals in a remarkable 4-2 win in Madrid just a few months after his £3 million move to Barcelona.

*Charlton striker Paul Williams gets in his header despite the efforts of Gary Pallister of Middlesbrough.*

# LONER NIGEL

## Soccer's quiet man set for Europe – if mum says it's OK!

**N**ottingham Forest's £2 million rated striker Nigel Clough is one player who really does let his feet do the talking.

In complete contrast to his extrovert manager and father Brian, 23-year old Nigel is as shy and modest as it is possible for such a gifted individual to be.

He shuns publicity and praise in the same calculated manner he uses to avoid tackles on the field where he now has a growing reputation as one of the most accomplished players in English football.

Possibly because of the outspoken brashness of his famous dad, the boy Nigel refuses to conduct press interviews, although he did break his vow of silence after last season's Littlewoods Cup Final victory over Luton.

Scorer of two goals in the 3-1 win and voted Man of the Match, he was called on to say a few words in front of the TV cameras. Somewhat reluctantly and with more than a little embarrassment, he agreed.

Blessed with such a reserved personality, it is difficult to imagine how, should he ever use his immense footballing talent to gain fame and wealth on the Continent, he will cope with the flood of publicity such a move would create.

Time and again he has been linked with Europe's top clubs and it is surely only a matter of time before Forest are tempted by a seven-figure offer.

According to dad, however, the lad is going nowhere.

In a typical Clough interview the Forest manager revealed that it was Nigel's mother who has the final say on the future of their gifted son.

"Any decisions concerning the family are down to the wife," explained Clough senior. "If she says he's not going abroad then he's not going abroad."

Among his City Ground team-mates Clough junior, who still lives with his parents in their Derbyshire home, is recognised as something of a loner, rarely mixing with his colleagues outside the work environment.

### Relationship

It is difficult to picture scenes inside the Clough household and even more so to hazard a guess as to the type of father-son relationship Brian and Nigel enjoy.

In public the unpredictable father refuses to even mention Nigel's name, referring to him as either 'the number nine' or 'the young centre-forward'.

As a player Nigel is anything but introvert and he is already following in the goalscoring footsteps of his father. Not as prolific, but undoubtedly with more all-round ability.

In just five years Clough has blossomed into a First Division player of the highest quality and utmost intelligence. Academically he was a bright boy at school and he is now developing into one of the most thoughtful players in the game.

His vision and perception, coupled with his all-round ability and instinct as a striker, are admired nationwide.

Called up to the full England squad for the first time for the game against Albania in April and awarded his first cap against Chile in May, it won't be long before he is banging in the goals for his country with the same consistency he has shown at club level.

He made his debut in a 2-0 win against Ipswich on Boxing Day, 1984, scoring his first goal some months later against Watford. In his first full season in the senior side (1985-86) he topped the Forest scoring charts with 18 League and Cup goals.

Top scorer again last season with more than 20 goals in all competitions, he is now well on his way to his first ton.

# MIDLANDS

ARTHUR COX

BRIAN CLOUGH

JOHN SILLETT

## Snoz and the gang hunt the Red Army

A motley collection of men called 'Mad Arthur', 'Ol' Big Head' and 'Snoz' are doing their bit to restore pride to Midlands soccer.

As managers of Derby, Forest and Coventry they are hell bent on breaking Merseyside's domination of the First Division Championship.

Not since 1981 – when Aston Villa borrowed the title for a year – has a team from outside Liverpool landed English soccer's premier prize. And that makes the terrible trio mad.

And all three – Mad Arthur (alias Arthur Cox), Ol Big Head (Brian Clough) and Snoz (John Sillett) – have vowed to do something about it next season.

If their efforts over the past 12 months are anything to go by neither will be too short of the mark.

Cloughie's brilliant young Forest side made the bravest assault on the 1988/89 Championship, only to slip out of the title race on the last lap. But they'll be back, young man.

The City Ground club served notice of their growing potential by lifting the Littlewoods Cup and making their mark in the ill-fated FA Cup competition.

Victory over Luton in the Final of the Littlewoods Cup last March gave Cloughie his first trophy for nine years.

In his first five seasons at Forest the outspoken boss had led his side to two European Cup triumphs, one League Championship title, two League Cup successes – and victory in the 1980 European Super Cup just for good measure.

But since then the cupboard has been bare at the City Ground – until the Littlewoods Cup came along.

The Wembley triumph must have brought memories flooding back for the game's greatest character. Memories, no doubt, of the glory days less than 20 miles down the road at the Baseball Ground.

It was as an enthusiastic young manager that Cloughie began to develop a reputation in the game at Hartlepool. And while he was later to achieve notoriety as a result of a 44-day stint at Leeds, it is in the Midlands that he's found fame ... and fortune.

As manager of Derby in the late 60s

Arthur Cox after winning the Second Division title in 1986.

# MEN of WAR

Flying Keith Houchen scores against Spurs in the 1987 FA Cup Final.

and early 70s he took the club into the First Division and within three years had led them to the Championship before leaving his team in the hands of Dave Mackay.

By the time Mackay was celebrating a similar managerial triumph in 1975, Clough was laying the foundations for future success at the City Ground, Nottingham.

While he was accumulating trophies and accolades as if they were going out of fashion, his old club Derby had past their peak and were proceeding at a rate of knots down the other side.

They had suffered the indignity of relegation to the Third Division before The Cox turned the ship round and began to steer the club along a more prosperous note.

Forest win the 1989 Littlewoods Cup.

## Top flight

Arthur Cox took charge at Derby in June 1984; three years later Derby were back where they belonged – in the First Division.

The club's first season back in the top flight was a tough one; a learning process not just for his team but Cox as well. A few shrewd buys, however, and an application of the coaching skills he has acquired since he was forced to quit the playing game at 18 have put the Rams firmly back on the soccer map.

He's not won the First Division Championship, yet, but in many ways he has done more for the modern Derby than Clough achieved in his time at the Baseball Ground.

And now 'King Arthur' will be doing his best to keep Cloughie in the shade

by making his team, not just number one in the Midlands but in the country as a whole.

That too is the aim of another of Midland soccer's great characters, John Sillett.

He has been the life and soul of Coventry City since the 1986-87 season when, together with his partner in crime George Curtis, he led his team in a merry dance around Wembley clutching the FA Cup.

Snoz promised to lead the club on to greater things and, while City have yet

to make an honest threat on the Championship Merseyside boasts as its own, the ambition remains.

For much of last seaason Coventry were rarely, if ever out of the top eight in the First Division and they now seem firmly established as a top flight force to be reckoned with. Much of that is down to John Sillett.

Like Mad Arthur and Ol Big Head, Snoz has instilled a belief and pride in his players that must surely stand all three managers – and their respective clubs – in good stead for years to come.

# Hoot!

"Excuse me. When you have finished signing autographs, would you mind taking the corner-kick?"

## THE TOP TEN FOOTBALL CLICHES

1. Over the moon
2. Sick as a parrot
3. It's a funny game
4. We just take each game as it comes
5. It was a game of two halves
6. Now we can concentrate on the League
7. It's an uphill battle from now on
8. I'm speechless, Brian!
9. The mud's a great leveller
10. The game could have gone either way

## Whatsaname

Rearrange these letters to reveal the name of a First Division defender:

**RAY VIDEOLAD**

Clue: He is a veteran in the Gunners' defence.

## IN A TANGLE

Can you untangle these letters to identify a Welsh international?

## MAKE A MATCH

*Can you match the international stars listed on the left with the countries they represent listed on the right? Award yourself a passmark in this nickname game if you can guess five or more?*

| | |
|---|---|
| 1. Careca | A: USSR |
| 2. Zubizarreta | B: Uruguay |
| 3. Soren Lerby | C: Argentina |
| 4. Antonio Sousa | D: Denmark |
| 5. Vassil Rats | E: Mexico |
| 6. Francescoli | F: Spain |
| 7. Joel Bats | G: Belgium |
| 8. Jorge Valdano | H: France |
| 9. Enzo Scifo | I: Portugal |
| 10. Hugo Sanchez | J: Brazil |

## Flashback

The heaviest player to appear in the Football League was a goalkeeper named Billy 'Fatty' Foulke who played for Sheffield United and Chelsea and weighed in at 21 stone. He also won an international cap for England. True or false?

## ASK THE EXPERT

### WHERE'S BOROUGH?

R. BELLION, of Walton-on-Thames in Surrey, is interested to know about what happened to Borough United – the "unknown" little club who bravely qualified as the Welsh representatives for the 1963-64 European Cup-Winners' Cup.

Sad to say, they are no more. The Welsh FA tell us the club – from Llandudno Junction, a small North Wales railway town with a population of around 2,000 – folded very shortly after their sensational, if brief, moment of glory in the national headlines.

Then – playing their home legs at Wrexham – they beat Sliema Wanderers of Malta 2-0 on aggregate, before losing 0-4 on aggregate to the powerful Czech side, Slovan Bratislava.

# WHO SAID IT?

*These are five quotes from famous football personalities. You pass the test if you can correctly guess three or more:*

1. "My only thought was to reach the free-kick and get a touch on the ball. I never dreamt of scoring the winning goal in an FA Cup Final. It was a memorable day for everyone involved with Wimbledon."
a) Lawrie Sanchez; b) Dennis Wise; c) Terry Gibson

2. "Throwing the ball at the referee was a stupid thing to do but I was so frustrated with our performance that I lost control. It was a vital World Cup match and we should have beaten Morocco. The ref was right to send me off and I regret the whole incident."
a) Steve Hodge; b) Kenny Sansom; c) Ray Wilkins

3. "Moving from Oxford to Derby has really helped my career. The whole set up at the Baseball Ground suits me and I fitted in with their playing style almost immediately."
a) Dean Saunders; b) Paul Goddard; c) Mark Wright

4. "It was a tough game in Albania. No international game is easy and it was a great relief to win. It was an added bonus that I managed to head the second goal."
a) John Barnes; b) Bryan Robson; c) Chris Waddle

5. "Howard Kendall is a tough act to follow. But I feel that with the purchase of quality players like Tony Cottee and Pat Nevin I have every chance of succeeding."
a) Ray Harford; b) Graham Taylor; c) Colin Harvey

# SNAPSHOTS

Bryan Robson, desperate to win his place back, offers manager Alex Ferguson his opinion: "Our number seven's not doing too well, is he?"

Norwich striker Robert Fleck is asked when he last scored a goal.

# 10 things you didn't know about IAN SNODIN

1. Ian was born in Thrybergh near Rotherham on August 15th, 1963.
2. As a boy, he supported Chelsea and his hero was 'Blues' striker Peter Osgood.
3. His favourite current player is Manchester United and England captain Bryan Robson, who Ian describes as the complete midfield player.
4. The biggest influences on his career are his father and Billy Bremner who managed him in his early career at Doncaster Rovers and Leeds United.
5. His most memorable match was for Doncaster Rovers against his current side Everton in the FA Cup in 1984. Everton won 2-0.
6. His favourite other sports are golf, cricket and badminton and the sportsman he most admires is Spanish golfer Severiano Ballesteros. Ian is also a keen follower of Rugby League and his favourite team are Doncaster.
7. He admits to being a telly addict and his favourite programmes are Only Fools And Horses and EastEnders.
8. His favourite actor and actress are Charles Bronson and Meryl Streep.
9. Ian is a keen music fan and likes most chart music. His favourite artists are George Benson and Big Country.
10. His main ambition in football is to play a major part in helping Everton to win the League Championship in the near future.

"Bert likes me to dress-up to watch the Cup Final on TV"

# What next...?

Barcelona, managed by Terry Venables, finished deadlocked at 0-0 with Steaua Bucharest after extra-time in the 1986 European Cup Final in Seville. The two teams then took part in a penalty shoot-out. Can you guess what happened next?

Hoot!

# BEASANT'S AROUND

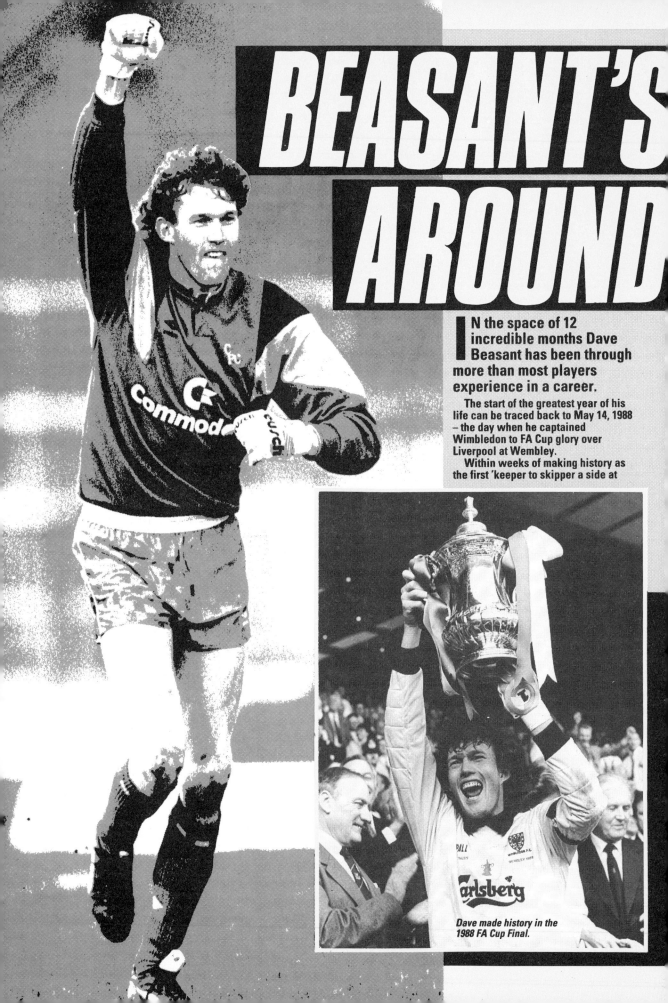

**I**N the space of 12 incredible months Dave Beasant has been through more than most players experience in a career.

The start of the greatest year of his life can be traced back to May 14, 1988 – the day when he captained Wimbledon to FA Cup glory over Liverpool at Wembley.

Within weeks of making history as the first 'keeper to skipper a side at

*Dave made history in the 1988 FA Cup Final.*

# BEEN

Wembley – and save a penalty in the process – he was re-writing the record books again.

When he joined Newcastle for £850,000 last summer he became the most expensive goalkeeper in British soccer history. Little more than six months later he was on the move again.

Joining Second Division Chelsea may have been seen as a gamble, but if it was it paid off in sensational fashion when he celebrated winning the championship and securing a prompt return to top flight action.

Amidst all that Beasant, who also earned a call-up to the England squad, wrote another memorable chapter into one of soccer's great success stories.

When Chelsea visited The Hawthorns, home of West Brom, on April 8, 1989 Beasant became the only current player to have appeared at all 92 League grounds.

"In actual fact I've played at 93," he points out. "I played at Newport's ground before they went out of the League and I also visited Scarborough's for a friendly after they'd clinched promotion to the Fourth Division in the summer of '87."

Wimbledon's Plough Lane was the scene for his League debut – and a game against Blackpool he'll never forget. "We lost 2-1 and I had a nightmare," he recalls.

## Groan goal

"I let their winning goal in through my legs and, as I was only in the team for the suspended Ray Goddard, I remember thinking to myself 'well, that's the end of my career as a professional goalkeeper'."

Of course, it wasn't and Beasant has gone on to play on every League ground. Technically speaking, however, he has still to play at Scunthorpe's new Glanford Park and Bristol Rovers' adopted home in Bath – Twerton Park.

"I did play on their old grounds so I'm sure that counts," adds Beasant

who lists White Hart Lane as his favourite ground. "Wimbledon always seemed to do well there and it was on Tottenham's ground that we beat Luton to reach the FA Cup Final.

"I was never that keen on Northampton's ground – there was never any atmosphere because the ground was too open with the cricket pitch on one side – and Maine Road always seems to have been a jinx venue for me."

One of his funniest experiences on an away ground was at Hartlepool 'many moons ago'.

"I was used to having things thrown at me from the crowd – apple cores, hot dogs, that sort of thing – but that was the first time I'd had a Mars Bar hit me," he recalls.

"For a laugh I picked it up, turned to thank the supporters and put it inside my glove bag…much to their amusement.

"I never thought any more of it until a few minutes later when I heard this huge roar – well as huge as they can make at Hartlepool – from behind the goal and when I looked round a little lad was rifling my glove bag.

"There was about £50 worth of gear in the bag, but all he wanted was the Mars Bar back. I couldn't believe it."

# BEASANT: THE FAX

Here, in chronological order, are the grounds Dave Beasant has played at – complete with the dates and scorelines:-

| Ground | Date | Opponents | Score |
|---|---|---|---|
| 1 Plough Lane | Jan 12, 1980 | Blackpool | 1-2 |
| 2 Brisbane Road | Aug 18, 1981 | Orient | 1-0 |
| 3 Roots Hall | Aug 24, 1981 | Southend | 2-1 |
| 4 County Ground | Aug 29, 1981 | Swindon | 1-4 |
| 5 Recreation Ground | Sep 1, 1981 | Aldershot | 0-0 |
| 6 Leeds Road | Sep 12, 1981 | Huddersfield | 1-1 |
| 7 Fellows Park | Sep 26, 1981 | Walsall | 0-1 |
| 8 Eastville Stadium | Sep 29, 1981 | Bristol R | 2-2 |
| 9 Sincil Bank | Oct 10, 1981 | Lincoln | 1-5 |
| 10 Elm Park | Oct 24, 1981 | Reading | 1-2 |
| 11 Fratton Park | Nov 3, 1981 | Portsmouth | 0-1 |
| 12 Turf Moor | Nov 7, 1981 | Burnley | 2-2 |
| 13 Recreation Ground | Nov 28, 1981 | Chesterfield | 0-2 |
| 14 Ashton Gate | Jan 2, 1982 | Bristol C | 3-1 |
| 15 Belle Vue Ground | Jan 29, 1982 | Doncaster | 3-1 |
| 16 London Road | Feb 3, 1982 | Peterboro | 1-0 |
| 17 Craven Cottage | Feb 9, 1982 | Fulham | 1-4 |
| 18 Priestfield | Feb 13, 1982 | Gillingham | 1-6 |
| 19 The Den | Feb 24, 1982 | Millwall | 1-2 |
| 20 St. James Park | Mar 20, 1982 | Exeter | 1-2 |
| 21 Sealand Road | Mar 31, 1982 | Chester | 1-1 |
| 22 Deepdale | Apr 3, 1982 | Preston | 2-3 |
| 23 Blundell Park | Apr 6, 1982 | Grimsby | 2-3 |
| 24 Home Park | Apr 14, 1982 | Plymouth | 0-2 |
| 25 *Somerton Park | Apr 17, 1982 | Newport | 0-0 |
| 26 Griffin Park | Apr 26, 1982 | Brentford | 3-2 |
| 27 Brunton Park | May 1, 1982 | Carlisle | 1-2 |
| 28 Manor Ground | May 15, 1982 | Oxford | 3-0 |
| 29 Selhurst Park | Aug 17, 1982 | C. Palace | 0-1 |
| 30 Boothferry Park | Sep 4, 1982 | Hull | 1-1 |
| 31 Bloomfield Road | Sep 18, 1982 | Blackpool | 1-1 |
| 32 Prenton Park | Oct 2, 1982 | Tranmere | 2-0 |
| 33 Bootham Crescent | Oct 16, 1982 | York | 4-1 |
| 34 Layer Road | Nov 2, 1982 | Colchester | 0-3 |
| 35 Victoria Ground | Nov 6, 1982 | Hartlepool | 0-1 |
| 36 County Ground | Nov 20, 1982 | N'thampton | 2-2 |
| 37 Feethams | Dec 4, 1982 | Darlington | 2-0 |
| 38 Spotland | Dec 11, 1982 | Rochdale | 2-0 |
| 39 Vale Park | Dec 18, 1982 | Port Vale | 0-1 |
| 40 Old Show Ground | Jan 29, 1983 | Scunthorpe | 0-0 |
| 41 Plainmoor | Feb 5, 1983 | Torquay | 1-0 |
| 42 Edgeley Park | Mar 11, 1983 | Stockport | 3-1 |
| 43 Field Mill | Apr 5, 1983 | Mansfield | 2-2 |
| 44 Edgar Street | Apr 16, 1983 | Hereford | 4-1 |
| 45 Gresty Road | Apr 30, 1983 | Crewe | 2-0 |
| 46 The Shay | May 10, 1983 | Halifax | 1-1 |
| 47 Gigg Lane | May 14, 1983 | Bury | 3-1 |
| 48 Burnden Park | Aug 27, 1983 | Bolton | 0-2 |
| 49 City Ground | Oct 26, 1983 | Nott'm For | 1-1 |
| 50 Springfield Park | Nov 12, 1983 | Wigan | 2-3 |
| 51 Millmoor | Nov 29, 1983 | Rotherham | 0-1 |
| 52 Valley Parade | Jan 7, 1984 | Bradford | 2-5 |
| 53 Dean Court | Mar 31, 1984 | Bournem'th | 3-2 |
| 54 Bramall Lane | May 5, 1984 | Sheff. Utd | 2-1 |
| 55 Turf Moor | May 12, 1984 | Burnley | 2-0 |
| 56 St. Andrews | Sep 1, 1984 | Birmingham | 2-4 |
| 57 Gay Meadow | Sep 15, 1984 | Shrewsbury | 2-1 |
| 58 Ayresome Park | Sep 18, 1984 | Middlesboro' | 4-2 |
| 59 Ewood Park | Sep 29, 1984 | Blackburn | 0-2 |
| 60 Molineux | Nov 17, 1984 | Wolves | 3-3 |
| 61 Elland Road | Dec 1, 1984 | Leeds | 2-5 |
| 62 Ninian Park | Dec 15, 1984 | Cardiff | 3-1 |
| 63 Goldstone Ground | Dec 29, 1984 | Brighton | 1-2 |
| 64 Boundary Park | Jan 1, 1985 | Oldham | 1-0 |
| 65 Maine Road | Jan 19, 1985 | Man. City | 0-3 |
| 66 Upton Park | Mar 6, 1985 | West Ham | 1-5 |
| 67 Brunton Park | Mar 23, 1985 | Carlisle | 1-6 |
| 68 Meadow Lane | Apr 6, 1985 | Notts Co. | 3-2 |
| 69 The Valley | Apr 13, 1985 | Charlton | 1-0 |
| 70 Oakwell | May 6, 1985 | Barnsley | 0-0 |
| 71 Carrow Road | Oct 5, 1985 | Norwich | 2-1 |
| 72 Victoria Ground | Oct 25, 1985 | Stoke | 0-0 |
| 73 White Hart Lane | Nov 6, 1985 | Tottenham | 0-2 |
| 74 Roker Park | Nov 9, 1985 | Sunderland | 1-2 |
| 75 Vicarage Road | Sep 6, 1986 | Watford | 0-1 |
| 76 St. James' Park | Sep 21, 1986 | Newcastle | 0-1 |
| 77 Abbey Stadium | Sep 23, 1986 | Cambridge | 1-1 |
| 78 Loftus Road | Oct 11, 1986 | QPR | 1-2 |
| 79 Highfield Road | Oct 19, 1986 | Coventry | 0-1 |
| 80 Stamford Bridge | Dec 6, 1986 | Chelsea | 4-0 |
| 81 Goodison Park | Dec 20, 1986 | Everton | 0-3 |
| 82 Highbury | Jan 1, 1987 | Arsenal | 1-3 |
| 83 Filbert Street | Feb 7, 1987 | Leicester | 1-3 |
| 84 Villa Park | Mar 4, 1987 | Aston Villa | 0-0 |
| 85 Anfield | Mar 28, 1987 | Liverpool | 2-1 |
| 86 Kenilworth Road | Apr 4, 1987 | Luton | 0-0 |
| 87 The Dell | Apr 7, 1987 | S'thampton | 2-2 |
| 88 Old Trafford | May 2, 1987 | Man. United | 1-0 |
| 89 Hillsborough | May 9, 1987 | Sheff. Wed | 2-0 |
| 90 Seamer Road | May 13, 1987 | Scarborough | 1-0 |
| 91 Baseball Ground | Aug 29, 1987 | Derby | 1-0 |
| 92 Portman Road | Mar 28, 1989 | Ipswich | 1-0 |
| 93 The Hawthorns | Apr 8, 1989 | West Brom | 3-2 |

*Newport now out of League

# Strachan LEEDS the way

**L**eeds United's determination to once again become a major force in European football can be proved by one name: Gordon Strachan.

The tricky Scottish international winger's arrival from Manchester United just before last season's transfer deadline was proof enough that the Yorkshire club are driven by their desire to recapture the glory days of Don Revie's magnificent team.

And not only because of Strachan's undoubted ability. Leeds, frankly, paid a fortune to get the man they wanted.

Strachan was also tracked by Sheffield Wednesday. Their manager Ron Atkinson, who had first signed Strachan more than six years ago from Aberdeen, offered the player the best personal terms he had ever been able to. Yes, even more than Bryan Robson first earned when he became a £1.5 million Atkinson signing.

But it was still nothing like the £250,000 two-year contract Leeds were prepared to offer to bolster their promotion plans. If Leeds are successful the contract could be worth up to a staggering £340,000.

Strachan duly signed, but not just for the money. "I don't fancy hanging around in the Second Division for long," he said after putting pen to paper last March.

"My ambition is to help Leeds get back into the top flight where they belong."

Leeds manager Howard Wilkinson sees the busy Strachan as United's modern-day Billy Bremner. And he forms an exciting midfield unit alongside Republic of Ireland ace John Sheridan and former England Under-21 star Vince Hilaire.

## Fan fare

No wonder so many football fans flock to Elland Road – a fact recognised and admired as far afield as London, where Chelsea's Kerry Dixon says: "United's crowds are fantastic. I have always believed that clubs with support such as Leeds deserve to be in the First Division."

It is a view shared by United striker Ian Baird, who says: "Our supporters are the best in the land. We are told that Manchester United and Liverpool have the greatest supporters but once we get success in the First Division we will be equal to them.

"Billy Bremner said recently that the fans are more fanatical at Elland Road now than they were during his playing days at the club in the 60s and 70s.

"And that is incredible when you take into account the disappointments they have had to endure over recent years."

Fans from all over the country flock to Elland Road.

Even boss Wilkinson, a man with almost 30 years experience in the game stretching back to his playing days with Sheffield Wednesday and Brighton, is staggered by the club's support.

But perhaps the best news of all is the hope that the club's hooligan element, which for so long blackened the club's name, is a thing of the past.

MERVYN
DAY
LEEDS

## DAVID McCREERY

**League Debut for Manchester United v Portsmouth (away), October 15, 1974.**

Manchester United were in the Second Division at the time, but, as usual, a large following of fans travelled to watch the Red Devils, which only added to the excitement of David McCreery, just 17 at the time.

"I was tremendously thrilled because I was on the substitutes' bench for this match and I was still only an apprentice," he recalls.

"I came on for Willie Morgan. It's all a bit vague, but I remember we drew 0-0 and that we went on to win the Second Division title that year.

"Our team at that time included Alex Stepney, Sammy McIlroy, Steve Coppell and many other household names."

David went on to collect an FA Cup Winners medal when United beat Liverpool 2-1 in a classic Final in 1977, a year after receiving a runners-up medal, and continued his fine career with QPR and Newcastle.

He sees similarities between his own circumstances and those of the crop of talented youngsters currently at Old Trafford.

"I look at players like Russell Beardsmore and think they will have a great opportunity at United, just like I did," he says.

Within two years of making his debut, David won his first Northern Ireland cap.

"I went on as substitute at Hampden Park against Scotland in a British Championship game. It was a great place to start, even though we lost 0-3. The roar from the crowd was deafening.

"My full international debut was in Northern Ireland's next game in the Championship against England at Wembley. We lost 0-4 and I felt absolutely drained."

Despite those two defeats, David was launched on an international career that has brought him more than 60 caps and seen him appear in the Finals of the 1982 and 1986 World Cups.

"I feel very privileged to have done that," says David.

# DAZZLING DEB

## PAUL RIDEOUT

**Italian Debut for Bari v Campobasso (home), August 1985.**

Paul started his football career at Swindon Town before moving on to Aston Villa, where he made his name as an exciting young striker.

In the summer of 1985, Paul joined his Villa team-mate Gordon Cowans in an £850,000 double move to the Southern Italian club Bari.

He found it quite a contrast to the city of Birmingham.

"My debut was in the equivalent of our League Cup, which is played before the League programme begins in Italy," says Paul.

"It was very hot even though we played at nine o'clock at night and the atmosphere was great. Bari had just been promoted after 16 years in the Second Division and there were almost 50,000 people there.

"I played up front and had a striking partner, which I quite often didn't have in Italy. We won 1-0."

Paul didn't score on that occasion, but was twice on target when he returned to England at the beginning of the 1988/89 season and made his debut for Southampton.

And he is justifiably proud of a personal record.

"I have never been on the losing side on any debut," he says.

David McCreery (left), still going strong for Newcastle United.

# UTS

## JOHN SCALES

**League Debut for Bristol Rovers v Newport County (away), September 7, 1985.**

A Wimbledon Wembley hero in 1988, began his Football League career in more humble surroundings, at Somerton Park, the home of Newport County, now sadly no longer in the League.

"I had been released by Leeds United after I had had a three month trial and Bristol Rovers gave me my first chance," says John.

"It was a Division Three game and I played at right back. We lost 0-3. I don't remember the crowd being very large."

In fact it was just 2,775 and the defeat left Bristol Rovers at the foot of the Third Division.

Yet Rovers recovered and avoided relegation and John impressed his manager, one Bobby Gould, so much that he played another 28 games in that

season of 1985/86.

"The game at Newport was quite a contrast to my first game for Wimbledon," says John. "It was our opening First Division game of the 1987/88 season and we were playing Watford at Vicarage Road. There were 15,000 people in the ground and, although the pitch was a bit bumpy, it was a good game.

"I was marking Luther Blissett and although he scored it wasn't my fault.

"The goal came from a corner and I still remember the inquests among our team. Watford won 1-0."

Bobby Gould, who bought John from Rovers, picked him for Wimbledon's next game, against Everton at Plough Lane, and he went on to share in a marvellous season which culminated in the FA Cup Final victory over Liverpool.

## TONY GALVIN

**League Debut for Tottenham Hotspur v Manchester City (home), February 3, 1979.**

"We lost 0-3, but it was our first season back in the First Division and were trying to consolidate our position," says Tony.

"Keith Burkinshaw was the manager then. I remember playing on the right wing and I was marked by Paul Power."

Manchester City finished 15th in the First Division that season despite having the likes of Colin Bell, Mick Channon and Joe Corrigan playing for them.

"I played quite well in that debut game," Tony recalls. "But I was disappointed with myself for being booked after I fouled Colin Bell because he was one of my heroes."

Tony made another 200 League appearances for Spurs and won two FA Cup winners medals and played in the UEFA Cup Final triumph against Anderlecht in 1984.

# THE LESSON FOOT

**A look at the way our national game is progressing towards the 21st Century. By SHOOT columnist JIMMY GREAVES**

**P**eople have said that after the Hillsborough disaster football can never be the same again. I just hope that they're right.

For I have a horrible vision of football in the future. And it's not a dream ... it's a nightmare!

Without wishing to sound like an old fogey, the game has deteriorated dramatically in the past 25 years or so. And unless that decline is halted, soccer is going to be something to be avoided instead of enjoyed.

When I was a kid I used to idolise the likes of Len Shackleton, Tom Finney and Stanley Matthews. They were skilful, exciting and entertaining.

Now it's Vinny Jones who is football's number one pin-up. The kids think he's great because he's got a skinhead haircut and steams into tackles like a Sunday League footballer.

And the danger is that more and more players are going to emulate his style until football will be virtually indistinguishable from rollerball.

For those of you too young to know what I'm on about, Rollerball was a 1970's science fiction film about a futuristic sport in which the primary aim was to take out the entire opposition in order to score the winning goal. There were no rules and the more violent the action, the more the spectators loved it.

But it seems that today's crowds have become so conditioned to a lack of real skill and excitement that they have turned to the cloggers to provide their entertainment.

That's why Vinny has become such a cult figure. He's the realisation of every schoolboy's dream of the park player who goes on to win the Cup at Wembley.

But I'm afraid that is not good enough any more. We need real heroes again, players like Georgie Best and Denis Law who could make your spine tingle with the pure genius of their play.

## Great skill

That's why I've been so encouraged by the form of Fat Boy Gascoigne. He's got great skill and he's a crowd pleaser. If he can replace Vinny as soccer's main man, that would be a step in the right direction.

The problem is that today's players don't want to accept any responsibility for the future of the game. They don't seem to realise that every provocative gesture to the crowd, every refused autograph and every unsavoury nightclub incident drags the image of the game down that little bit more.

Not that all football's problems can be attributed to the players. Because the bulk of the blame for the state of the modern game lies at the door of the administrators.

It's ludicrous to have two separate organisations running the game. The Football League and the FA should be merged, with an on the ball character like the PFA chief Gordon Taylor in charge.

If the League clubs were organised properly they could become one of the most powerful group of employers in the country.

The number of people employed by the 92 teams – players, managers and coaches, ground staffs, secretarial and administration workers and catering staffs – must be close on 10,000. If they were all to present a united front to the Government, Maggie and Colin Moynihan wouldn't dare to trample all over the game in the current fashion.

## Greed

But the problem is that there is so much greed in the game that clubs are stabbing each other in the back in order to grab a bigger slice of the cake for themselves.

That's why I am so opposed to the creation of a Superleague. At the moment there are powerful men

# ALL HAS TO LEARN - FAST

*Above: Vinny Jones ... in trouble again.*

plotting a breakaway of the elite clubs, which will be great for the chosen few but will leave the rest struggling for survival.

There is enough money to go around, but the smaller clubs must stop expecting hand outs from the big boys and learn to stand on their own two feet.

I'm not in favour of the 16 richest teams going it alone, but I can understand their resentment at constantly having to subsidise the lame ducks. If clubs cannot survive without charity they must give way to the ambitious, well-organised non-League teams who would be only too willing to take over.

And the first thing that needs to be sorted out is the modernisation of our grounds.

It's ironic that at a time when yuppies are paying fortunes to live in Victorian houses, our football stadia were virtually all built in the 19th Century.

But the chances of the chinless wonders handing over their millions for our grounds are virtually nil. And I can't say I blame them.

After all, who wants to stand with a bunch of yobboes on filthy, uncovered terraces, queue half an hour for a disgustingly wet hot dog and then do the breaststroke in order to go to the toilet?

The Hillsborough disaster has had such a profound effect on the fans that they are finally waking up to the fact that they have been cruelly taken advantage of.

Now they are demanding decent facilities, comfort and entertainment. And if their demands aren't met, they'll finally turn their back on their game for good.

The League constantly points to the fact that gates have shown a marginal increase in the last couple of years, but the clientele they are are attracting is all wrong.

At the moment football appeals almost exclusively to young men who tolerate the bad language and the jostling which has given the game such a bad image.

The families aren't going to come back in any great numbers while the yobs are still dominating the scene, and although I'm not mad on the idea of handing over vast areas of our stadiums for executive boxes, that could be the only way ahead.

Your average terrace supporter hates the idea of rich businessmen sitting in their glass boxes watching TV and knocking back the scotch and sandwiches.

But these people are paying through the nose for the privilege and should be encouraged to keep coming rather than sneered at.

## Salvation

Because it's big business which is going to prove the game's salvation. It's already started with shirt sponsorship and if our soccer clubs can forge a friendly relationship with booming local businesses that is one obvious source of finance for the building of completely new stadia.

I'd love to see a new national stadium built to replace Wembley. Ideally, it would be in the heart of the country, with easy access for everybody instead of just the Londoners.

The NEC in Birmingham is ideally positioned, it has motorways, rail links and an airport all on its doorstep and would be the perfect site for a new all-seater stadium which would stand comparison to Munich's magnificent Olympic Stadium.

The 21st Century is almost with us, but football is still living in the Victorian age. Either it moves with the times or it dies!

*The game needs heroes like Denis Law.*

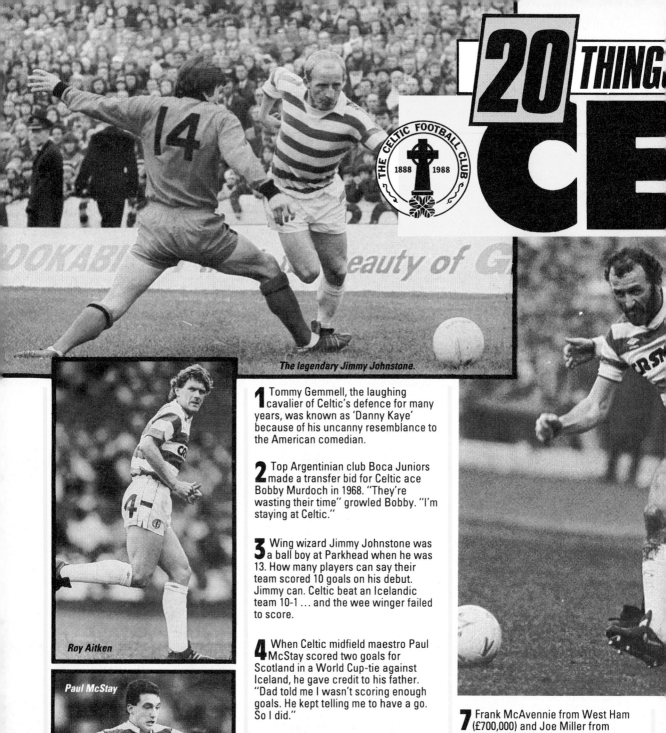

The legendary Jimmy Johnstone.

Roy Aitken

Paul McStay

**1** Tommy Gemmell, the laughing cavalier of Celtic's defence for many years, was known as 'Danny Kaye' because of his uncanny resemblance to the American comedian.

**2** Top Argentinian club Boca Juniors made a transfer bid for Celtic ace Bobby Murdoch in 1968. "They're wasting their time" growled Bobby. "I'm staying at Celtic."

**3** Wing wizard Jimmy Johnstone was a ball boy at Parkhead when he was 13. How many players can say their team scored 10 goals on his debut. Jimmy can. Celtic beat an Icelandic team 10-1 … and the wee winger failed to score.

**4** When Celtic midfield maestro Paul McStay scored two goals for Scotland in a World Cup-tie against Iceland, he gave credit to his father. "Dad told me I wasn't scoring enough goals. He kept telling me to have a go. So I did."

**5** Danny McGrain overcame injury and illness to become Celtic's greatest right-back. He fractured his skull playing against Falkirk; doctors discovered he had diabetes, and then he was ruled out for a full year after a full-blooded collision with his friend John Blackley, of Hibs. He survived it all to win his 62nd and final Scotland cap against Russia in the 1982 World Cup Finals.

**6** Former Celtic manager Jock Stein watched Celtic Boys' Club in action to offer glowing reports on a robust 13-year-old. "That boy will play for Scotland" promised Stein. He had been watching Roy Aitken.

**7** Frank McAvennie from West Ham (£700,000) and Joe Miller from Aberdeen (£650,000) came close to completing their first season as Celts without suffering defeat. Celtic's remarkable run of 31 games without loss was broken by Hearts, who beat them 2-1.

**8** When ex-Celtic striker Charlie Nicholas returned to Parkhead for a pre-season friendly with his new club Arsenal, he was roundly booed by the crowd. Charlie said later: "That really got to my Dad. I don't think he's been back to Parkhead since that day."

**9** Jock Stein wanted Charlie Nicholas to join Liverpool *not* Arsenal. He favoured Liverpool because he felt the discipline and professionalism at Anfield would be good for Charlie.

# OU DINNAE KEN ABOOT
# LTIC

*Kenny Dalglish*

*Former skipper Danny McGrain.*

**15** Former Celtic ace Kenny Dalglish is joint record goal-scorer for Scotland with 30. He shares the honour with Denis Law. Dalglish made a record 102 appearances for Scotland between 1971-86.

**16** Celtic equalled the record they already shared with Dundee United for most goals in a Premier Division season when they scored 90 in 44 games in 1986-87.

**17** Four Celtic players have won the Scottish PFA's 'Player of the Year' award in the 1980s. They are Davie Provan (1980), Charlie Nicholas (1983), Brian McClair (1987) and Paul McStay (1988).

**18** Celtic's triumphant manager Billy McNeill was on the dole for the first time in his life when sacked by Aston Villa. "That's football" said the man christened 'Caesar' by the Parkhead fans.

**19** Celtic goalkeeper John Thomson, who, at only 21, became Scotland's goalkeeper, threw himself at the feet of Rangers' striker Sammy English in the Old Firm battle of September 1931. Thomson was stretchered off, to die six hours later in Glasgow's Victoria Infirmary. He was just 23 years old.

**20** Celtic played their first game on May 28, 1888 against ... yes, Glasgow Rangers. In the early days, they invited English clubs to play them at Parkhead. Sunderland, Everton, Bolton, Burnley, Preston, Wolves, Notts County, Aston Villa and Blackburn all went to Glasgow.

**10** Billy McNeill's 486 League appearances between 1957-75 is a club record.

**11** Record attendance at Parkhead is the 92,000 gate that watched Celtic v Rangers on New Year's Day 1938.

**12** Motherwell sent Celtic crashing to their heaviest (8-0) defeat in April 1937.

**13** Jimmy McGrory is Celtic record goal-scorer. He scored 397 goals for them between 1922-39.

**14** A record European Cup attendance of 135,836 watched Celtic play Leeds in the semi-finals at Hampden Park on 15 April, 1970.

*Jimmy McGrory*

*Frank McAvennie*

**G**oal-machine Keith Edwards is out on his own as the Football League's leading marksman with more goals to his credit than any other current player.

Quite an achievement when you realise the 32-year-old striker had to think long and hard before deciding to quit his job to try his luck in football.

"It was a labouring job, nothing special but secure," recalls the goalmouth assassin. "From that point of view football was a gamble, because all I was offered was a three-month trial."

A Sheffield United scout liked the look of the 18-year-old with an obvious eye for goal, but Edwards remembers being apprehensive when he was asked to go on trial at Bramall Lane.

"I was knocking in a few goals for a local youth side back home on Teesside, but to be honest the standard wasn't all that high," he explains.

# GOAL-KING EDWARDS

"Then, all of a sudden, I was being asked to join a First Division club.

"It worked out well for me, of course, although I was disappointed when the club was relegated in my first season there. The sum total of my First Division career is three games and no, I didn't score in any of them."

Edwards is in his second spell with Hull City, his first being sandwiched between two stints with Sheffield United, during which time he won two SHOOT/adidas Golden Shoe Awards in 1982 and 1984. And his other ports of call were Leeds and Aberdeen.

It was Ian Porterfield, his former boss at Bramall Lane, who took him North of the border to Pittodrie, but he cut short his stay in Scotland after failing to become a regular choice.

He had a similar problem at Elland Road, although his goals helped Leeds to the FA Cup Semi-Finals in 1987 when it needed extra time to separate them from eventual winners Coventry City.

And Edwards played his part in steering Leeds into the promotion play-offs when they came within a whisker of returning to the First Division that same year.

"People have always asked if I would have scored goals at the top level and I must admit I'd have liked the chance to find out," he says.

"When you look at my record I'm confident I could have done it in the First Division.

"There were times, earlier in my career, when I used to think to myself 'Surely a First Division club will come in for me now' but it never happened. Apparently there was plenty of interest but nothing came of it.

## No regrets

"But I don't want to sound bitter because I really don't have any complaints or regrets about the way things have gone for me in football."

Edwards was delighted when Hull were paired with Liverpool in last season's FA Cup. "I'd have hated to have gone through my career without playing against them," he explains.

"And even though we lost 3-2 to them I had a reason to celebrate. I scored one of our goals and that created my best-ever sequence of scoring in eight successive games!"

King Edwards is adamant that there's still plenty of power left in his shooting boots and promises further goals before he hangs them up.

"I still enjoy my football and that's the most important thing of all. And I'm very proud of my record. It never occurred to me when I hesitated about taking up Sheffield United's offer all these years ago that I would one day become the League's top scorer."

KEVIN WILSON

CHELSEA

## 1980

**LEAGUE CHAMPIONS:** Liverpool
**FA CUP:** West Ham United
**LEAGUE CUP:** Wolves
**EUROPEAN CUP:** Nottingham Forest
**CUP WINNERS' CUP:** Arsenal beaten on penalties by Valencia
**INTERNATIONAL SCENE:** West Germany win the European Championship by beating Belgium 2-1 in the final. England fans disgrace themselves by rioting in Turin.
**MANAGERIAL MERRY GO-ROUND:** Mike England is appointed manager of Wales. Johnny Giles resigns as Eire boss.
Malcolm Allison sacked by Man. City. John Bond leaves Norwich to take over at Manchester City.
Terry Venables moves from Crystal Palace to QPR. Malcolm Allison is appointed manager of Crystal Palace.
**TRANSFER TRAIL:**
Garry Birtles – Nottingham Forest to Manchester United – £1,500,000
Clive Allen – QPR to Arsenal – £1,250,000. Kevin Reeves – Norwich to Man. City – £1,000,000
Steve Archibald – Aberdeen to Spurs £1,000,000
**OBITUARY:**
Manchester United chairman Louis Edwards dies of a heart attack. Everton legend Dixie Dean dies at Goodison Park. He was 72.
Alan Hardaker, Director General of the Football League, dies of a heart attack at 67.
Former FA chairman Sir Andrew Stephen dies.
**TRAGEDIES:**
Two die when a gate collapses at a match between Middlesbrough and Manchester United.
**MISCELLANEOUS:**
Eamon Collins, at 14 years 323 days, becomes the youngest player to appear for a League club when he comes on as substitute in an Anglo-Scottish Cup tie against Kilmarnock.

*Trevor Brooking scores with a rare header as West Ham win the FA Cup in 1980.*

## 1981

**LEAGUE CHAMPIONS:** Aston Villa
**FA CUP:** Tottenham
**LEAGUE CUP:** Liverpool
**EUROPEAN CUP:** Liverpool
**UEFA CUP:** Ipswich Town
**MANAGERIAL MERRY GO-ROUND:**
Geoff Hurst sacked by Chelsea.
Howard Kendall leaves Blackburn to take over as manager of Everton.
Preston sack Tommy Docherty.
**TRANSFER TRAIL:**
Bryan Robson – WBA to Man. Utd. – £1,500,000. (New British record).
Trevor Francis – Nottingham Forest to Manchester City – £1,200,000.
Justin Fashanu – Norwich to Nottingham Forest – £1,000,000.
Frank Stapleton – Arsenal to Manchester United – £900,000.
**OBITUARY:**
Bill Shankly dies, aged 67.
Former Burnley chairman Bob Lord dies, aged 93.

*Tommy Docherty – sacked as manager of Preston after 17 games.*

# FA<br>DE

## 1983

**LEAGUE CHAMPIONS:** Liverpool
**FA CUP:** Manchester United
**LEAGUE/MILK CUP:** Liverpool. Bob Paisley collects the trophy on his last visit to Wembley as Liverpool manager.
**CUP-WINNERS' CUP:** Aberdeen
**MANAGERIAL MERRY GO-ROUND:**
Bob Paisley retires as Liverpool manager. Joe Fagan takes over.
John Greig resigns at Rangers.
John Toshack resigns at Swansea.
Jock Wallace takes charge at Rangers for a second time.
Arsenal sack Terry Neill. Coach Don Howe takes over.
John Toshack is re-appointed as Swansea manager.
**TRANSFER TRAIL:**
Luther Blissett – Watford to AC Milan – £1,000,000.
Charlie Nicholas – Celtic to Arsenal – £750,000.
**OBITUARY:**
Former FA Secretary Sir Denis Follows dies aged 72.
Andy Beattie, former Scotland manager, dies aged 70.
**MISCELLANEOUS:**
Only 24,000, the lowest Wembley crowd ever, turn out to see England beat Wales.
Spurs beat Nottingham Forest 2-1 in the first Sunday afternoon 'live' TV game.

## 1982

**LEAGUE CHAMPIONS:** Liverpool
**FA CUP:** Tottenham
**LEAGUE CUP:** Liverpool
**EUROPEAN CUP:** Aston Villa
**INTERNATIONAL SCENE:**
Italy win the World Cup in Spain with a thrilling 3-1 final victory over West Germany.
**MANAGERIAL MERRY GO-ROUND:**
Tony Barton is appointed manager of Aston Villa after a spell as caretaker following Ron Saunders' resignation.
Malcolm Allison takes over as manager of Middlesbrough.

## 1984

**LEAGUE CHAMPIONS:** Liverpool – only the third club in history to win the First Division three years in succession.
**FA CUP:** Everton
**LEAGUE/MILK CUP:** Liverpool after a replay against Everton.
**EUROPEAN CUP:** Liverpool defeat AS Roma 4-2 on penalties.
**UEFA CUP:** Tottenham Hotspur beat Belgium club Anderlecht 5-4 in a penalty shoot-out.
**INTERNATIONAL SCENE:**
Northern Ireland win the final British Championship after 100 years of competition between the four home countries.
John Barnes scores a sensational solo opening goal as England beat Brazil 2-0 in Rio.
France, inspired by captain Michel Platini who scores nine goals in five matches, win the European Championship with a 2-0 victory over Spain in Paris.
**TRANSFER TRAIL:**
Ray Wilkins – Man. Utd to AC Milan – £1,500,000.
Mark Hateley – Portsmouth to AC Milan – £915,000.
Diego Maradona – Barcelona to Napoli – £6,000,000.

George Graham is appointed manager of Millwall.
Bobby Robson succeeds Ron Greenwood as England manager.
**TRANSFER TRAIL:**
Trevor Francis – Manchester City to Sampdoria – £900,000
Liam Brady – Juventus to Sampdoria – £780,000
Kevin Keegan – Southampton to Newcastle – £100,000
**OBITUARY:**
Arsenal chairman Denis Hill-Wood dies.
**MISCELLANEOUS:**
At 17 years 42 days, Norman Whiteside becomes the youngest player ever to appear in the World Cup Finals. Pele was the previous record holder at 17.

**MANAGERIAL CHANGES.**
Terry Venables leaves QPR to join Barcelona.
Arthur Cox quits newly promoted Newcastle United for Third Division Derby.
Keith Burkinshaw resigns at Spur after winning the UEFA Cup.

**RETIREMENTS:**
Newcastle United and former England striker Kevin Keegan, 33, after leading the club back to the first Division. Keegan also played for Scunthorpe, Liverpool, Hamburg SV and Southampton in a career spanning 15 years.
Trevor Brooking, 35, after 19 years service with his only club West Ham.

*Continued over page*

## 1985

**LEAGUE CHAMPIONS:** Everton
**FA CUP WINNERS:** Manchester United. Kevin Moran becomes the first player to be sent-off in an FA Cup Final.
**LEAGUE/MILK CUP:** Norwich City
**CUP WINNERS' CUP:** Everton beat Rapid Vienna 3-1
**MANAGERIAL MERRY GO-ROUND:**
Kenny Dalglish is appointed player-manager of Liverpool.
Jim Smith leaves Oxford, who he has taken from the Third Division to the First in successive seasons, for QPR.
**TRANSFER TRAIL:**
Gordon Cowans/Paul Rideout – Aston Villa to Bari – £850,000 combined
Gary Lineker – Leicester to Everton – £800,000
**OBITUARY:**
Harry Catterick, former Everton player and manager, collapses and dies at Goodison Park. He was 65.
Scotland manager Jock Stein collapses and dies of a heart attack after the Scotland-Wales World Cup-tie.
**TRAGEDIES:**
Fifty-six fans die when a fire sweeps through the main stand at Bradford City's Valley Parade ground.
On the same day, 15-year-old schoolboy Ian Harridge is killed when Leeds United fans riot at Birmingham City.
Thirty-eight people are killed when a wall collapses after rioting by Liverpool fans before the Liverpool-Juventus European Cup Final at the Heysel Stadium, Belgium. The game was held up by 90 minutes and the fighting that occurred resulted in an indefinite ban on English clubs in European competition. Juventus won 1-0.
**MISCELLANEOUS:**
Trevor Francis is given the kiss of life following a clash of heads while playing for Sampdoria.
During an FA Cup tie between Luton and Millwall, the referee has to take the teams off the pitch for 25 minutes while the police fight a pitch battle with Millwall fans.
Charlton Athletic move to Selhurst Park and share the ground with Crystal Palace.

You're off! In 1985 Manchester United's Kevin Moran was the first ever player to be dismissed in an FA Cup Final.

Ray Houghton blasts Oxford's second in the 1986 Milk Cup Final win over QPR.

## 1986

**LEAGUE CHAMPIONS:** Liverpool – Player-manager Kenny Dalglish scores the winning goal against Chelsea as they clinch the title.
**FA CUP:** Liverpool – Kenny Dalglish becomes the first player-manager in history to win the 'double'.
**MILK CUP:** Oxford United.
**INTERNATIONAL SCENE:**
England reach the World Cup Quarter-Finals in Mexico before going out to the eventual winners Argentina in controversial circumstances. Diego Maradona scores both goals in Argentina's 2-1 win, the first of which was with his hand. England's Gary Lineker is the competition's top scorer with six goals.
**TRANSFER TRAIL:**
Mark Hughes – Manchester United to Barcelona – £2,300,000
Ian Rush – Liverpool to Juventus – £3,200,000 (New British record fee)
Gary Lineker – Everton to Barcelona – £2,750,000
Chris Woods – Norwich to Rangers – £600,000
Terry Butcher – Ipswich to Rangers – £750,000
**MANAGERIAL CHANGES:**
Graeme Souness (£300,000 from Sampdoria of Italy) becomes player-manager of Rangers.
Jack Charlton replaces Eion Hand as manager of the Republic of Ireland.
George Graham moves from Millwall to take over at Arsenal.
David Pleat is appointed at Spurs.
Manchester United sack Ron Atkinson and appoint Alex Ferguson, from Aberdeen, as manager.
**OBITUARY:**
Sir Stanley Rous, 91 – President of FIFA from 1961-74.
**MISCELLANEOUS:**
Luton Town are expelled from the 1986-87 Littlewoods Cup because of their ban on visiting fans.

*Mirandinha.*

# 1987

**LEAGUE CHAMPIONS:** Everton
**FA CUP:** Coventry City – the club's first major honour.
**LEAGUE/LITTLEWOODS CUP:** Arsenal
**UEFA CUP:** Dundee United are beaten by Gothenburg (2-1 on aggregate)
**INTERNATIONAL SCENE:**
England win 4-2 in a friendly against Spain with Lineker scoring all four.
The Football League beat the Rest of the World 3-0 at Wembley in a game to celebrate the Football League's centenary season.
England beat Yugoslavia 4-1 in Belgrade to qualify for the European Championship Finals in West Germany.
**TRANSFER TRAIL:**
Glenn Hoddle – Spurs to Monaco – £750,000
Mark Hateley – AC Milan to Monaco

– £1,000,000
Peter Shilton – Derby to Southampton – deal worth £1,000,000
Mirandinha – Palmeiras to Newcastle – £575,000 (the first Brazilian to play in the Football League)
Ruud Gullit – PSV Eindhoven to AC Milan – £6,000,000
**MANAGERIAL CHANGES:**
Howard Kendall leaves Everton for Athletic Bilbao in Spain.
Terry Venables quits as manager of Barcelona after three defeats in their opening four games.
**MISCELLANEOUS:**
The first Football League promotion/relegation play-offs take place.
Barclays Bank take over sponsorship of the Football League (worth £4.5 million over 3 years).
GM Vauxhall Champions Scarborough are promoted to the Fourth Division in place of Lincoln City who lose their League status.

*England stunned. Underdogs Eire win 1-0 in 1988 European Nations Cup.*

*Never forget... the horror of Hillsborough as 95 die in the semi-final crush.*

# 1988

**LEAGUE CHAMPIONS:** Liverpool
**FA CUP WINNERS:** Wimbledon.
Liverpool's John Aldridge becomes the first player to miss a penalty in an FA Cup Final.
**LEAGUE/LITTLEWOODS CUP:** LUTON.
**INTERNATIONAL SCENE:**
England suffer a dreadful European Championship. They are beaten in all three of their first round games – by the Republic of Ireland, Holland and Russia – and are knocked out of the tournament. The Republic put up a brave fight but they too are finally eliminated by Holland, who go on to win the competition.
**MANAGERIAL MERRY GO-ROUND:**
Dave Bassett is appointed manager of Sheffield United.
Tommy Docherty resigns at Altrincham after four months.
John Hollins leaves Chelsea after an "amicable discussion".
Former Liverpool and Republic of Ireland defender Mark Lawrenson, who was forced to retire through injury, is

appointed manager of Oxford United.
Bobby Campbell takes over as manager of Chelsea.
**TRANSFER TRAIL:**
Ian Ferguson – St Mirren to Rangers – £850,000 (a new Scottish record fee)
Dave Beasant – Wimbledon to Newcastle – £850,000 (a new British record fee for a goalkeeper).
Mark Hughes – Barcelona to Manchester United – £1,500,000
Paul Stewart – Manchester City to Spurs – £1,700,000
Paul Gascoigne – Newcastle to Spurs – £2,000,000 (a British record fee)
Tony Cottee – West Ham to Everton – £2,200,000 (a British record fee)
Gary Stevens – Everton to Rangers – £1,000,000
Clive Allen – Spurs to Bordeaux – £1,000,000
**MISCELLANEOUS:**
Rangers' Terry Butcher and Chris Woods are fined £500 and £250 respectively after being found guilty of disorderly conduct and breach of the peace during a Rangers-Celtic match.
Peter Shilton breaks Terry Paine's League appearance record with his 825th appearance in Derby's 1-1 draw with Watford.

# 1989

**LEAGUE CHAMPIONS:** Arsenal
**FA CUP:** Liverpool
**LEAGUE/LITTLEWOODS CUP:**
Nottingham Forest – Brian Clough's first major honour in nine years.
**INTERNATIONAL SCENE:**
Maurice Johnston breaks Denis Law's all-time World Cup scoring record for Scotland with his eighth goal in the 2-1 win over Cyprus at Hampden Park.
**TRANSFER TRAIL:**
Mel Sterland – Sheffield Wednesday to Rangers – £800,000
Frank McAvennie – Celtic to West Ham – £1,250,000
**TRAGEDY:**
Ninety-five people die and 170 are injured at the beginning of the Nottingham Forest-Liverpool FA Cup semi-final.
**MISCELLANEOUS:**
Non-League Sutton United provide one of the biggest shocks in FA Cup history when they beat First Division Coventry 2-1 in the Third Round. GM Vauxhall Champions Maidstone elected to League in place of Darlington.

Charlton were four minutes away from relegation when up stepped Peter Shirtliff to equalise and then the defender scored a last minute winner (above) to give his side a 2-1 win against Leeds in the play-off Final.

BELOW: Paul Miller heads the precious equaliser in Charlton's 1-1 draw with Chelsea to condemn the Stamford Bridge club to the play-offs and ultimately relegation in the 1987-88 season.

*The*

RIGHT: Carl Leaburn scores Charlton's winner against Wimbledon last season in a vital 1-0 victory for the Selhurst Park club.

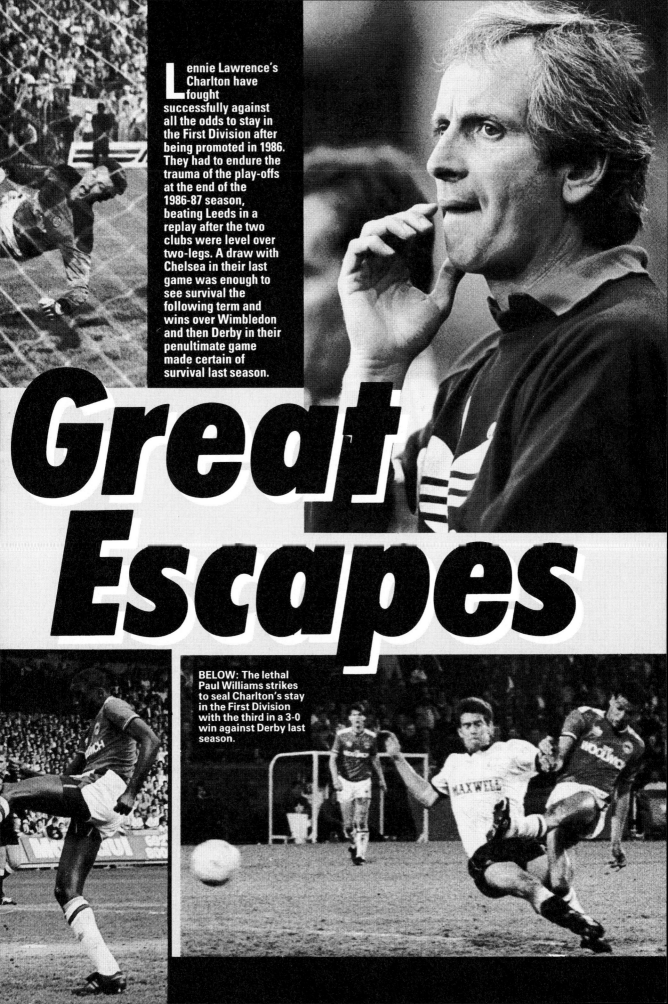

**L**ennie Lawrence's Charlton have fought successfully against all the odds to stay in the First Division after being promoted in 1986. They had to endure the trauma of the play-offs at the end of the 1986-87 season, beating Leeds in a replay after the two clubs were level over two-legs. A draw with Chelsea in their last game was enough to see survival the following term and wins over Wimbledon and then Derby in their penultimate game made certain of survival last season.

# Great Escapes

BELOW: The lethal Paul Williams strikes to seal Charlton's stay in the First Division with the third in a 3-0 win against Derby last season.

# NO FUSS

*Narey made the headlines with a World Cup cracker against Brazil in 1982.*

**S**eventeen years and more than 700 games ago, Jim McLean made his first signing as a manager without even seeing the player in action.

The Dundee United supremo – he's also Chairman at Tannadice – took something of a gamble when he acted on the advice of a scout to snap up a local schoolboy.

But the risk factor was soon removed as McLean quickly realised he had unearthed a gem of a player in Dave Narey.

Within six months of signing a professional contract on his 17th birthday, Narey was making his debut. Now at 33, he has established an appearance record that might never be broken.

No wonder McLean insists: "No player has contributed more to the good times at Tannadice than Dave. His efforts on behalf of the club have been nothing short of magnificent.

"No one has to tell me how fortunate I was to sign him all those years ago. It's true I had never seen him play. For all I knew, he could have had a wooden leg!"

It was when the shrewd McLean heard Narey was about to head South

of the border for a trial with Nottingham Forest that he pounced to keep him in his native Dundee.

He's been there ever since, of course, despite many attempts to lure him to England. Tottenham, Derby, Southampton and Leeds all offered big money – and all were turned down.

Celtic also wasted their time with a transfer bid as home-loving Narey opted to stay put and create one long-playing record after another.

Apart from playing more games than any other player in United's history, he is also the club's most capped player. Indeed, before Narey's international debut as a substitute against Sweden, in April, 1977, no United player had ever earned the cap call.

The modest defender reached another milestone when he played his 70th European game for United, surpassing the achievment of Billy McNeill, now the Celtic boss, when he was a Parkhead player.

Narey also graduated to the Tannadice captaincy, but such is his desire to stay out of the limelight that only a few weeks after taking charge he was asking to be relieved of his duties.

"I just like to get on with my football with the absolute minimum of fuss," he explains. "It's just the way I am."

It is thanks to Narey's remarkable consistency, alongside a string of other long-serving Tannadice stalwarts, that United have been such a force at home and abroad over the years.

# NAREY

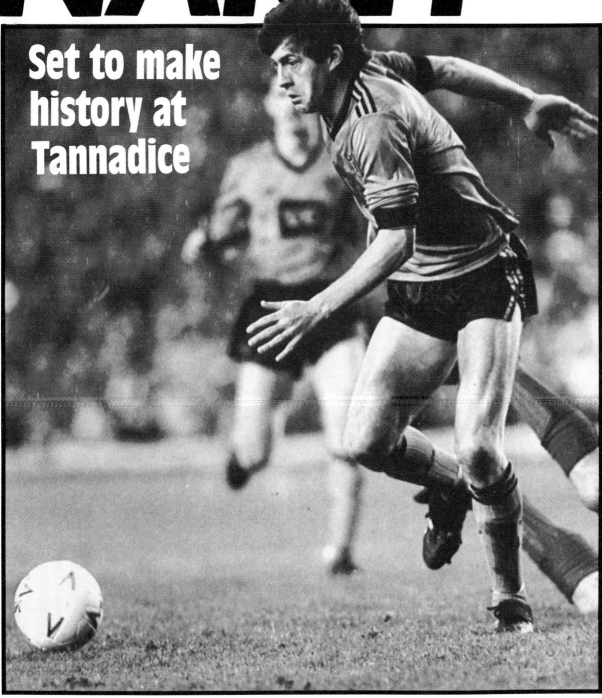

## Set to make history at Tannadice

His form last season, when he earned a surprise recall to the Scotland scene, was as good as ever and manager McLean was quick to offer him an extension to his contract.

It seems Narey's familiar role at the heart of the Tannadice defence is assured for some time to come – and his love affair with football seems set to continue after he eventually hangs up his boots.

He admits: "Earlier in my career I had no real desire to continue in the game when my playing days were over.

"But now I view things differently. I've been fortunate enough to have earned a living from a job I've thoroughly enjoyed all the way through, so I'm hoping to stay in football in some capacity.

"I don't want to talk about retiring just yet, however. I've got three or four years left and I want to make the very best of them."

# WHEN BRITAIN REIGNED IN EUROPE

**E**NGLISH clubs' continuing exile from Europe is costing them valuable experience and revenue. It is also devaluing the competition because hardly a season went by in recent years without a British club winning one of the three European trophies. SHOOT! decided to take a look back at what we, the Government and the rest of Europe, are missing.

*Steve Chalmers scores the winner for Celtic in 1967.*

# Super Celts

## EUROPEAN CUP:

**1967 – CELTIC 2 INTER MILAN 1 (LISBON)** – Britain's first winners of the European Cup were Celtic, and they achieved that in 1967, beating Inter Milan 2-1. A goal down after only seven minutes, to Mazzola's penalty-kick, Celtic fought back to win with goals from Tommy Gemmell and Steve Chalmers.

**1968 – MANCHESTER UNITED 4 BENFICA 1 (AET, WEMBLEY)** – A year after Scottish club football's greatest day came England's. Manchester United became the first English club to win the European Cup with a stunning performance to defeat Portuguese Champions Benfica. Bobby Charlton opened the scoring after 55 minutes but Graca equalised with ten minutes of normal time remaining. However, just three minutes into extra-time, George Best waltzed through the Benfica defence to put United back in the lead, and further goals from Brian Kidd – on his 19th birthday – and Charlton secured a memorable victory.

**1977 – LIVERPOOL 3 BORUSSIA MOENCHENGLADBACH 1 (ROME)** – Kevin Keegan, in his last game for Liverpool before his £500,000 transfer to

*Liverpool after beating Roma on penalties in 1984.*

*Aston Villa celebrate in 1982.*

John Robertson's goal won the European Cup for Forest in 1980.

# crush Inter

Manchester United's fourth goal against Benfica.

SV Hamburg, inspired his team-mates to their first European Cup win. Goals from Terry McDermott, Tommy Smith and a Phil Neal penalty earned them the top prize in Europe. Allan Simonsen was Borussia's scorer.

**1978 – LIVERPOOL 1 BRUGES 0 (WEMBLEY)** – Liverpool became the first English club and only the sixth in history – joining Real Madrid, Benfica, Inter Milan, Ajax and Bayern Munich – to retain the European Cup. Kenny Dalglish, in his first season for Liverpool, scored the decisive goal early in the second-half.

**1979 – NOTTINGHAM FOREST 1 MALMO 0 (MUNICH)** – Forest kept the trophy in England for the third successive year thanks to a £1 million goal from Trevor Francis. That was the fee Brian Clough paid to Birmingham City to sign Francis in February and his headed goal – in his first European Cup match – paid off a substantial portion of that fee.

**1980 – NOTTINGHAM FOREST 1 HAMBURG 0 (MADRID)** – A raking drive from John Robertson kept Europe's greatest prize at the City Ground. Robertson broke away from his marker, Manfred Kaltz, and played a one-two with Garry Birtles before driving his shot in off the far-post.

**1981 – LIVERPOOL 1 REAL MADRID 0 (PARIS)** – Liverpool were made to battle hard, but in the end a rare goal from full-back Alan Kennedy, nine minutes from time, was enough.

**1982 – ASTON VILLA 1 BAYERN MUNICH 0 (ROTTERDAM)** – Aston Villa won the European Cup at their first attempt despite the handicap of losing goalkeeper Jimmy Rimmer through injury after only eight minutes. He was replaced by Nigel Spink, who had played just one senior game prior to the Final, but he performed superbly. The winning goal came from a Peter Withe tap-in.

**1984 – LIVERPOOL 1 AS ROMA 1 (ROME; LIVERPOOL WON 4-2 ON PENALTIES)** – Alan Kennedy, Liverpool's goalscoring hero in the 1981 European Cup Final, held his nerve in front of 50,000 partizan Italians to score the decisive penalty which clinched the trophy. Liverpool were leading 3-2 on penalties with one spot-kick remaining for each side when Kennedy stepped forward coolly to score and spark off tremendous celebrations among his team-mates. In normal time, Phil Neal had given Liverpool the lead, but Pruzzo equalised for the Italians.

# EUROPEAN CUP-WINNERS' CUP:

**1963 – TOTTENHAM HOTSPUR 5 ATLETICO MADRID 1 (ROTTERDAM)** – Tottenham became the first British club to win a European trophy with a sparkling performance in Rotterdam. Two goals apiece from Jimmy Greaves and Terry Dyson and one from John White completed a memorable night for Spurs and England.

*Continued overleaf*

# WHEN BRITAIN REIGNED IN EUROPE

**1965 – WEST HAM UNITED 2 TSV MUNICH 0 (WEMBLEY)** – Two goals in two minutes from Alan Sealey gave West Ham their greatest victory in front of a packed Wembley. Both sides squandered chances in the first-half, before the Hammers made the breakthrough in the 69th minute. Ronnie Boyce pushed the ball through for Sealey who drove home a powerful shot from a difficult angle. And two minutes later the game was won when Sealey scored after Munich's goalkeeper failed to collect Bobby Moore's free-kick.

**1970 – MANCHESTER CITY 2 GORNIK ZABRZE 1 (VIENNA)** – City claimed their only European trophy on a wet night in Vienna with a fine first-half performance, despite losing wing-half Mike Doyle with an ankle injury after only 16 minutes. By the interval, goals from Neil Young and Francis Lee (a penalty) had sealed the game.

**1971 – CHELSEA 2 REAL MADRID 1 (REPLAY, AFTER 1-1 AET, ATHENS)** – First-half goals from Peter Osgood and John Dempsey brought the Cup-Winners' Cup back to England for the second year running, despite a furious Real fightback. They pulled a goal back 15 minutes from time through Fleitas and stormed forward in search of an equaliser, just as they had done in the first match when Zoco equalised Osgood's goal with the last kick of the game. However, on the second occasion, Chelsea held firm to win.

**1972 – RANGERS 3 MOSCOW DYN. 2 (BARCELONA)** – Rangers became Scotland's first winners of the Cup-Winners' Cup in front of 20,000 of their own supporters, making it almost like a home match. Two goals from Willie Johnston and one from Colin Stein gave Rangers a 3-0 lead before Moscow Dynamo could get into the game. Naturally, as Rangers tired after their early efforts, Moscow hit back and scored through Eshtrekhov, on the hour, and Mahovikov, three minutes from time.

**1983 – ABERDEEN 2 REAL MADRID 1 (AET, GOTHENBURG)** – An extra-time goal by super-sub John Hewitt gave Aberdeen their first European trophy in their 80-year history and inflicted upon Real their first defeat by a Scottish side. Hewitt had come on as a substitute in the Quarter-Final against Bayern Munich and scored the winner. He repeated the trick after replacing Eric Black in the Final. Black had given Aberdeen the lead after only five minutes but Juanito responded with a penalty 16 minutes later.

Liverpool skipper Emlyn Hughes with the 1976 UEFA Cup.

Alan Sealey scores West Ham's second goal against TSV Munich.

# Reds rule supreme

**1985 – EVERTON 3 RAPID VIENNA 1 (ROTTERDAM)** – Everton added the Cup-Winners' Cup – their first European trophy – to the League Championship they had won nine days before with a splendid performance. Vienna, who had angered Europe by demanding – and being granted – a replay against Celtic in the second round after claiming one of their players had been struck by a missile at Parkhead, got what they deserved – nothing. Andy Gray, Trevor Steven and Kevin Sheedy scored for The Toffees.

*Frans Thijssen helped Ipswich beat AZ67.*

*Above: Aberdeen win the Cup Winners' Cup. Left: Red hot Spurs.*

## FAIRS/UEFA CUP:

**1968 – LEEDS UNITED bt FERENCVAROS 1-0 on aggregate** – A solitary goal by Mick Jones, scored in the first-leg at Elland Road, was enough to give Leeds their first European trophy.

**1969 – NEWCASTLE UNITED bt UJPEST DOZSA 6-2 on aggregate** – 60,000 passionate Geordies were at St. James' Park for the first-leg to see Newcastle open up a commanding 3-0 lead. The second-leg was a dramatic occasion with Dozsa taking a two-goal lead, through Bene and Gorocs, and looking as though they would go on and win the trophy. However, Newcastle stuck by their attacking principles and were rewarded with goals from Moncur, Preben Arentoft and Alan Foggon to clinch victory.

**1970 – ARSENAL bt ANDERLECHT 4-3 on agg.** – Trailing 3-1 from the first-leg in Belgium Arsenal responded magnificently in front of 51,000 supporters at Highbury. Eddie Kelly opened the scoring in the 26th minute and John Radford and Jon Sammels sealed the game with two goals in the 73rd and 74th minutes.

**1971 – LEEDS UNITED bt JUVENTUS on away goals after 3-3 on agg.** – Leeds United claimed the Fairs Cup for the second time in four years. The first-leg in Turin finished 2-2 with Leeds twice coming from behind through goals from Paul Madeley and Mick Bates. The second-leg finished 1-1 with Leeds' goal being scored by Allan Clarke with Anastasi replying for Juventus.

**1972 – TOTTENHAM bt WOLVES 3-2 on agg.** – Tottenham became the first English club to win separate European competitions – adding the UEFA Cup to the Cup-Winners' Cup they won in 1963. Martin Chivers scored twice in the first-leg at Wolverhampton – whose scorer was Jim McCalliog – to set Spurs up for a glory night at White Hart Lane. It didn't quite go to plan but a 1-1 draw was enough for Spurs to take the magnificent trophy.

**1973 – LIVERPOOL bt BORUSSIA MOENCHENGLADBACH 3-2 on agg.** – By now the UEFA Cup was almost Britain's own property as Liverpool made sure that we kept the trophy for yet another season, thanks to their first leg performance at Anfield, which gave them a 3-0 lead to take to Germany. Kevin Keegan led the way with two goals and Larry Lloyd added the third.

**1976 – LIVERPOOL bt BRUGES 4-3 on agg.** – An incredible fightback in the first-leg at Anfield secured the trophy for Liverpool. They were 2-0 down after just 12 minutes after goals from Lambert and Cools but three goals in four second-half minutes – from Alan Kennedy, Jimmy Case and Kevin Keegan (penalty) – turned the tie back in Liverpool's favour. The second-leg finished 1-1 with Keegan again on target for Liverpool. Bruges' goal was a penalty by Lambert.

**1981 – IPSWICH TOWN bt AZ 67 ALKMAAR 5-4 on agg.** – A splendid first-leg performance at Portman Road against an uncompromising Dutch side made the UEFA Cup safe for Ipswich. John Wark opened the scoring with a penalty after 27 minutes. Within 11 minutes of the second half Ipswich had wrapped the game up with goals from Franz Thijssen and Paul Mariner. Ipswich lost 4-2 in the return but had done enough to win.

**1984 – TOTTENHAM bt ANDERLECHT 4-3 on penalties after 2-2 on agg.** – Goalkeeper Tony Parks won the UEFA Cup for Spurs in a dramatic penalty shoot-out. He saved the final penalty from Gudjohnsen to clinch the trophy and ensure an emotional farewell for manager Keith Burkinshaw in his last game in charge at White Hart Lane.

# When football
## DISASTERS THAT SHOCK THE SOCCER WORLD

**F**irst comes the shock, then the pain, then the anger – as football counts its dead. Football history has had its share of grim disasters, and Britain has suffered more than most...

### 1902                    April 5

Twenty-five people died and 500 others were injured when a stand collapsed at the Ibrox stadium in Glasgow during a Scotland-England international.

Many of the dead were crushed as panicking fans fled onto the pitch. Other victims plunged 50 feet to the ground when the wooden north-west terracing gave way.

Mounted police, unaware of what had happened, rode into the fleeing crowd, so the play continued despite the disaster.

As a result of the Ibrox disaster, all terracing in Britain was constructed of concrete.

### 1914                February 14

Seventy-five supporters were injured at Hillsborough, Sheffield when a retaining wall collapsed during a replayed F.A. Cup-tie between Sheffield Wednesday and Wolves.

The game resumed after the injured had been transported to city hospitals and Wednesday won 1-0.

### 1946                    March 9

Thirty-three fans died and 500 were badly injured when steel barriers collapsed at Burnden Park, Bolton after thousands of supporters had broken down fencing to get into a packed enclosure to watch the F.A. Cup-tie with Stoke City.

Police, who had closed entrance gates nearly an hour before the trouble, had been overwhelmed by the surging crowd who broke down perimeter fencing to get into the ground.

Several fans were crushed to death, but others were saved by police who tore down fencing to allow supporters to pour onto the pitch.

*Below: The horrible scene at Bradford and above, the fateful steps at Ibrox in 1961.*

# cried

A dangerously high figure of 65,000 had been allowed into the ground for the Sixth Round tie. The game was held up for 30 minutes and the players left the pitch.

Referee George Dutton decided the match should continue, a decision heavily criticised afterwards, but the full, sad circumstances of one of football's blackest days were not known to him at the time.

### 1949                                        May 14

The entire Torino team, including eight Italian internationals, were killed when the plane carrying the Italian League Champions crashed at Superga, outside Turin.

### 1958                                     February 6

The city of Manchester was plunged into mourning when the Elizabethan 'plane carrying Manchester United back from a European Cup Quarter Final tie in Belgrade crashed on take-off at Munich.

Its tyres never left the icebound tarmac. Instead of taking off, the aircraft sped through landing lights, an airport fence, and into a house 250 yards from the runway.

Roger Byrne, Geoff Bent, Eddie Colman, Mark Jones, David Pegg, Tommy Taylor and Liam Whelan died. Duncan Edwards fought against injuries but died a fortnight later in hospital.

John Berry and Jackie Blanchflower never played again. Ken Morgans, Albert Scanlon, Dennis Viollet, Ray Wood and Matt Busby, the Manager, were injured.

'The world wept for Manchester United. My life had been spared but I wanted to die' said Busby, in a vivid account of the nightmare in which 23 people died.

### 1961                                 September 16

Two people were killed and several injured when crash barriers collapsed at Ibrox stadium, Glasgow during an Old Firm game between Rangers and Celtic.

### 1964                                        May 24

The biggest disaster in the history of sport occurred at the National Stadium, Lima, Peru when 301 people were killed and more than 500 injured in a riot.

It started six minutes before the end of a match between Peru and Argentina when the referee

The despair of Hillsborough.

disallowed a goal by the home side.

Police used teargas on the rioters, and in their panic to get out of the stadium, many were trampled to death in the stampede.

### 1985                                        May 11

Fifty-two people were killed and more than 100 injured when fire swept through the packed main stand of Bradford City's Valley Parade ground.

Many deaths were caused by crushing and trampling as fans tried to escape the flames, which became a raging inferno.

Fans later expressed their concern over padlocked gates at the rear of the stand which prevented them from escaping. The gates were smashed down but the delay claimed many lives.

Before the fire, the crowd had been in buoyant mood, celebrating the club's promotion to the Second Division at their abandoned game that day against Lincoln City.

### 1985                                        May 29

Unbelievably, only days after the Bradford disaster, English football was plunged into mourning at the European Cup Final between Juventus and Liverpool at the Heysel Stadium, Brussels when a riot ended in tragedy with 39 people dead and more than 300 injured.

A television audience of millions witnessed a horror show in their own living rooms as Liverpool supporters clashed with Juventus fans.

A wall collapsed as Liverpool fans broke through a barrier to chase Juventus followers. Some died instantly beneath the debris and a

panic stricken crowd.

Never has the result of a major football Final meant less to the participants. Michel Platini scored, Juventus won, Liverpool lost, and nobody cared.

### 1989                                       April 15

Ninety-five people were crushed to death, many of them youngsters, and 200 injured at the F.A. Cup Semi-Final tie between Liverpool and Nottingham Forest at Hillsborough, Sheffield.

In the worst tragedy in British football history, the city of Liverpool was plunged into mourning for the second time in four years.

At 2.55 p.m., just five minutes before kick-off, a large gate at the Leppings Lane end of the ground was opened on the instruction of a senior police officer.

He had been worried that fans would be crushed in the build-up, swelled by fans without tickets, outside the ground.

Less than 60 seconds after the Gates of Hell opened, the first of the victims died, trampled to death as hundreds of fans swarmed onto the terracing.

Only when the full horror of the moment was evident was the match stopped. Even as the players left the pitch, a few minutes after kick-off the lucky ones were being lifted over the fencing that had become a prison of death for so many.

The Liverpool players attended a memorial service in Liverpool on the following night. An official week of mourning was declared for the city... and the world of football.

# FACTFILE
# RUUD GULLIT

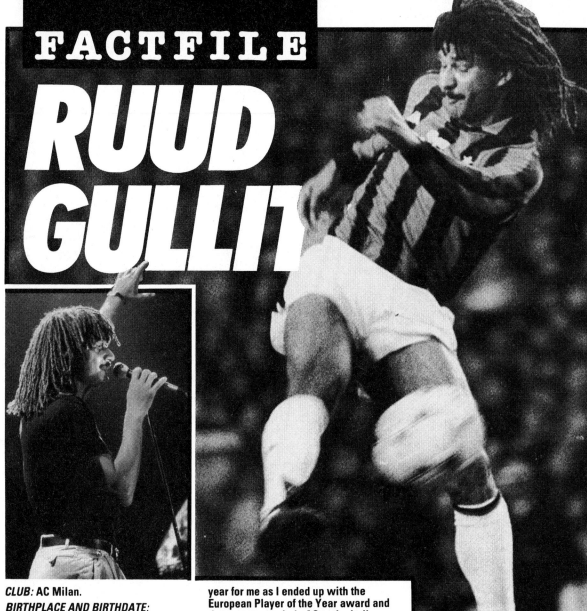

**CLUB:** AC Milan.

**BIRTHPLACE AND BIRTHDATE:** Amsterdam, September 1, 1962.

**HEIGHT AND WEIGHT:** 6ft 3in, 13st 10lbs.

**MARRIED:** To Yvonne. We have two daughters, Felicity Vanity and Sharmayne.

**HOME:** Seven bedroomed apartment with swimming pool just outside Milan.

**CAR:** Lancia Thema.

**CAREER DETAILS:** I started my soccer life at FA Haarlem in 1979 scoring 32 goals in 91 games for them and won my first international cap for Holland against Switzerland in 1981. I joined Feyenoord in 1982 (30 goals in 85 games) and helped them win the Cup and League double in 1984. A move to PSV Eindhoven followed in 1985 where I recorded my best scoring performance (46 in 68). We won the League Championship in 1986 and '87 and then I decided on a change of scenery and moved to AC Milan in 1987 for a £6 million fee. 1987 proved a good

year for me as I ended up with the European Player of the Year award and then went on to help AC to the Italian League title in the '87-'88 season. But the European Championships in Germany provided my greatest moment with Holland beating Russia 2-0 in the Final to clinch our first major trophy at international level. Last season proved another great success with my club winning the European Cup Final after our victory over Steaua Bucharest.

**HOBBIES:** Music. I sing and play bass guitar in a reggae band Revelation Time. We had a top ten hit in Holland with Not The Dancing Kind. I also enjoy a night out at a disco.

**POLITICS:** I'm a strong anti-apartheid supporter and a keen socialist. I once told the sponsors of PSV, electronics company Philips, that they should sell me and use the money to create more jobs.

**ON THE PARK:** The days of the truly individual footballer are over. The game is faster and results depend on groups of players although obviously Marco van Basten had a big say in

Holland's success in the European Championships. But even great players like Marco and Diego Maradona are not allowed to run the show especially in Italy where players are marked so tightly.

**THE BEST PLAYER IN THE WORLD:** Without doubt Diego Maradona. Everyone in football admires and respects his ability. Italy striker Gianluca Vialli is very useful and will be one to look out for in next summer's World Cup Finals, especially as they are in his own back yard. Liverpool's John Barnes is an incredible footballer who is strong and technically brilliant. He puts the fear in to any defence.

**DAVID SMITH**
**COVENTRY**

# It's so t

Tony made a dream start to his Everton career, scoring a hat-trick against Newcastle. Here's TC's second.

**J**oining Everton for a British record £2.2 million gave me the biggest thrill of my career. It also provided me with my greatest challenge.

As soon as I put pen to paper on a five year deal I placed my head firmly on the chopping block by announcing I will have scored 150 goals by the time the contract ends. At the time I felt that 30 goals a season was well within my reach but it didn't take long for me to realise I had set myself a daunting target. Here's how that first season at Goodison unfolded...

## AUGUST

The night before my League debut against Newcastle I dreamed of scoring the winner, so to hit three in a 4-0 win was out of this world. I had to wait just 34 seconds for my first goal and after an I hour I was on cloud nine when the third went in.

## SEPTEMBER

When I scored the only goal of the game at Coventry it seemed that life at the top was just plain sailing. As it turned out the sea got a bit rough and I didn't manage another goal that month.

## OCTOBER

Another defeat by a London side, Wimbledon, saw us slip to 10th in the table but we recaptured our opening day form a week later to beat Southampton 4-1 and again I was among the goals. I struck twice and my partnership with Graeme Sharp was starting to gel. After we'd been held 2-2 by Bury (we went through 5-2 on aggregate) and defeated 2-0 by Villa I was back on target against Man United, equalising a Mark Hughes special.

## NOVEMBER

Not a brilliant month by any means but it did have its good points, one being a victory at Upton Park. As expected I took quite a bit of stick from the West Ham fans so it was nice to come away with a 1-0 win. I can't remember the last time I was

so nervous before a game. We never lost at all during November but we were held to 1-1 draws by Sheffield Wednesday, Norwich and then Oldham in the Third Round of the Littlewoods. It wasn't until the replay at Boundary Park on the 29th that I scored my first goals of the month. I hit both in a 2-0 win.

## DECEMBER

The month started off superbly with me scoring my 100th senior goal in a 1-0 win over Spurs, and then sampling my first Merseyside derby as we drew 1-1 at Anfield. But on December 14 disaster struck when we were knocked out of the Littlewoods by Bradford. They were 3-0 up at half time and we were awful. Five days later we were in action in the Simod Cup in front of a massive crowd of 3,700! We beat Millwall 2-0 and I scored one.

## JANUARY

A 2-0 defeat by Forest left our title claims looking a bit sick so the FA

Cup took on a whole new importance. We needed an 86th minute goal by Kevin Sheedy in a Third Round replay to see off West Brom and we also took two matches to dispose of Plymouth in the Fourth Round. No goals for me this month.

## FEBRUARY

Vinny Jones and Wimbledon showed us the ugly side of soccer and I was glad to come out of our League match with them unscathed. Kevin Ratcliffe wasn't so lucky as he was butted by Jones who fully deserved his marching orders. The game ended in a 1-1 draw, as did the next match against Southampton when I was subbed in the second half after what was probably my worst performance of the season to date. I scored in the

# ough

next game against Villa (yet another 1-1 draw) and in the Cups we progressed to the Quarter Finals of the FA by beating Barnsley 1-0 and reached the Semis of the Simod.

## MARCH

The highlight of the month was without doubt our 1-0 win over Wimbledon in the Quarter Finals of the FA Cup. In the League I scored the winner against Sheffield Wednesday before we hit rock bottom with a 2-0 defeat at Newcastle. I was dropped for the Millwall match but came back to score in a 3-3 draw against Middlesbrough.

## APRIL

When we beat QPR 4-1 on April 1 it was only our second League win in 1989. I was on the mark again but a week later didn't get much of a look-in against Arsenal, the club some people say I should have joined. We lost 2-0 and The Gunners are going for the title but I know I made the right decision in joining Everton. Having said that I was dropped for the next match against Charlton and with the FA Cup Semis only a week away there was a danger I could miss the big one

against Norwich. Thankfully I didn't and we won 1-0 to book a place at Wembley – but it didn't seem to matter when we heard the tragic news from Hillsborough. Even losing the Simod Cup Final 4-3 to Forest (I scored twice) didn't hurt.

## MAY

A mixed month to say the least. We lost just one of our last five League games, and three consecutive victories against Manchester United, my old club West Ham and Derby sent us into our FA Cup Final clash with Liverpool full of confidence. For obvious reasons it was a very emotional occasion and was quite an experience for me playing in my first Wembley final. I'd played there for England but this was different. From a personal point of view I didn't have a good game, but when Stuart McCall equalised John Aldridge's opener in the dying seconds I thought the day was going to end on a high note. It didn't and we all know the reason why – Ian Rush.

*Tony Cottee*

# AWAY FROM OF THE

Arsenal's Paul Davis is the boss of The Eastenders.

Wayne Clarke is a keen golfer.

**B**eing a professional footballer can be a stressful business. So how do the players ease the pressures? Paul Gascoigne likes to fish and Vinny Jones enjoys shooting. SHOOT asks some other top players about their hobbies and pastimes.

PAUL DAVIS: Arsenal's midfield star is a fan of most sports. But did you know that he is also the manager of a London football team? Read on …

❝It is important for footballers to get away from the pressures of the game. But as soon as people find out what I do, the subject usually turns to football.

I do have another interest in the game, though, as manager of the 'Eastenders' football team. We play most Sundays and train once a week when we can.

The team which boasts such stars as Lofty (Tom Watt) and Wicksey (Nick Berry), play against local sides and other Showbiz elevens. All the money we raise goes to charity.

I do a variety of charity work, including visits to children's hospitals with the rest of the Arsenal team.

I also enjoy watching and playing many sports. These include: boxing, tennis, squash, badminton and cricket.❞

# THE ROAR CROWD

## HOW THE STARS RELAX

**WAYNE CLARKE:** The youngest member of the Clarke footballing dynasty, Leicester's Wayne is also one of football's many golfers.

❝For me there is nothing more relaxing than a round of golf. I've got a handicap of 12 and hope to be joining a club very soon.

Other golfing mates include: Kevin Ratcliffe, Graeme Sharp and Trevor Steven, and we have some very competitive games.

There are players who are always doing something connected with football. That doesn't mean they love the game any more than me. It's just that I prefer to get away from it sometimes.

### Long drive

Another hobby is driving. This is fortunate because I live in the Midlands and it's quite a long drive to play golf with my former Evertonians.❞

**BERNIE SLAVEN:** He may be the star of Middlesbrough's forwards, but for most of the time it's a dog's life for Bernie!

❝It is important to have other things in life to take your mind off football. A lot of players are into other sports like golf but I don't have sporty hobbies.

The two things that take up most of my time are my dogs. One is an Irish Setter and the other a stray which I found last winter. I came out of a shop one night and he was just standing there. I put notices in the papers but no-one claimed him.

I play a bit of tennis but I'm not very good; I'd prefer to be with the dogs.❞

**LEROY ROSENIOR:** West Ham's dynamic striker likes to play snooker or spend time with his two young sons. Here he reveals some more serious pastimes.

❝I agree that footballers should have interests outside the game. We get a lot of spare time and I think it's important to use that time constructively.

I'm trying to get involved in the black arts and am especially interested in

*Leroy Rosenior supports the black cause in South Africa.*

*Bernie Slaven enjoys a dog's life.*

helping the blacks in South Africa; mainly publicising their cause.

I sometimes help out with the sickle cell anaemia cause – a blood disorder which affects black people. Charlton's Garth Crooks does a lot of work here and we go to various charity presentations.❞

# ROBSON
# THE MASTER BLA

**B**ryan Robson has finally abandoned all hope of overtaking Bobby Charlton as the most prolific marksman in England's international history.

To achieve that place in the record books Robbo must score a cool 50 times for his country. And having taken 75 games to reach the halfway mark, the 32-year-old skipper of Manchester United accepts that he is now chasing Mission Impossible.

But that doesn't detract from the incredible achievement of England's Captain Fantastic who currently stands seventh in the list of England's all-time top scorers in spite of winning all his caps as a midfield player.

"My current striking record is about one goal in three games, but it could have been closer to one in two if I'd been given more attacking responsibilities," admits Robson.

"My barren spells for England have coincided with defensive roles in midfield, when Bobby Robson has asked me to do a holding operation.

"I've always got a real thrill out of scoring for my country and that's why I want to stay in midfield for as long as possible rather than drop back to sweeper as some people would prefer."

*Bryan strikes the first of his three goals against West Germany.*

But Robson is also honest enough to admit that his England goal account at the end of the 1988-89 season should actually have stood at 23 goals.

For he reveals: "My very first goal for England, against Norway in 1981, should have been disallowed.

"There was an awkward bounce and although I managed to chest it down I also used my hand to control the ball before belting it into the net. But the referee was on my blind side and didn't see the infringement. And I wasn't going to say anything!"

But if there was an element of luck about that goal, Robson has more than made up for it with some spectacular and vital strikes.

His most satisfying England goal? "The one I scored against East Germany in 1984 always sticks in my mind," Bryan admits.

# N STER

## ROBBO'S ENGLAND GOALS

| Date | Opponents + Venue | Res. | Goals |
|---|---|---|---|
| 9.9.81 | Norway (a) | 1-2 | 1 |
| 23.2.82 | N. Ireland (h) | 4-0 | 1 |
| 3.6.82 | Finland (a) | 4-1 | 2 |
| 16.6.82 | France (WC – Spain) | 3-1 | 2 |
| 1.6.83 | Scotland (h) | 2-0 | 1 |
| 16.11.83 | Luxembourg (a) | 4-0 | 2 |
| 12.9.84 | E. Germany (h) | 1-0 | 1 |
| 17.10.84 | Finland (h) | 5-0 | 2 |
| 14.11.84 | Turkey (a) | 8-0 | 1 |
| 12.6.85 | W. Germany (Mexico) | 3-0 | 3 |
| 16.10.85 | Turkey (h) | 5-0 | 1 |
| 26.2.86 | Israel (a) | 2-1 | 1 |
| 1.4.87 | N. Ireland (a) | 2-0 | 2 |
| 14.10.87 | Turkey (h) | 8-0 | 1 |
| 11.11.87 | Yugoslavia (a) | 4-1 | 1 |
| 15.6.88 | Holland (EC – W G'mny) | 1-3 | 1 |
| 8.2.89 | Greece (a) | 2-1 | 1 |
| 8.3.89 | Albania (a) | 2-0 | 1 |

*Robbo scores against Holland in June 1988.*

*His first for England v. Norway in Oslo 1981.*

"It was a long range half volley which could have ended up in the Wembley terraces, but instead flew into the top corner of the net. But it was so satisfying because I scored it with my right foot, and that's usually reserved for standing on.

"I got another one like that in Israel a couple of years later and netted my one and only penalty for England in that same game."

But in terms of importance, Robson singles out his World Cup goals against France, a vital strike in Yugoslavia and his brave solo effort in the 1988 European Championships against eventual winners Holland.

"Everyone remembers my goal against France during the 1982 World Cup finals in Spain because I scored the first after just 27 seconds, which is still a record for the tournament.

"Obviously it was a vital goal because it gave us just the spur we needed to go on and win 3-1.

"But in terms of execution, my second goal gave me a bigger thrill because it was probably the best header I've scored at international level.

"Another vital goal was that one in Belgrade a couple of years ago.

"We needed to avoid defeat by the Yugoslavs to make sure of qualifying for the European Championship finals, so it was quite a tense occasion.

"But Peter Beardsley calmed our nerves with a goal in the first couple of minutes and John Barnes grabbed another from a free-kick soon after.

"That's when I got in on the act with a solid left footer and after that I knew we were going to the finals.

Unfortunately, once out in West Germany for the Championship finals, things did not go according to plan.

A 1-0 defeat by Eire was followed by another dismal performance against the Dutch which ended English interest in the competition.

But a brave solo goal by captain Bryan had momentarily raised hopes and cancelled out Marco van Basten's first of three for the Dutch that day.

"I really thought we were going to go on and win from there, but we weren't able to sustain our game and in the end lost 3-1," says Bryan.

That result was a shattering blow for Bryan, but he has never been one to sulk and it didn't take him long to get back on the goal trail.

Further goals in Greece and Albania last season prove that even at 32 he has not lost the goal touch and all England hopes that there are still a lot more to come yet.

# THE YOUNG ONES

*Tony Gill – one of United's young versatile stars.*

## Manchester minors give City and United a lift

**N**ot since the days of the great Sir Matt Busby has there been such excitement around the Manchester area.

The young ones have arrived and sparked off a youthful revolution set to take the First Division by storm.

Few would argue that it was Manchester City who made their mark first on this occasion, but the teenage tornado which took the Blues back into the top section came from a blueprint used well before any of the young Maine Road stars were born.

The Busby Babes are a football legend.

They were created by Sir Matt and his right hand man Jimmy Murphy in the early 1950s when United dominated the FA Youth Cup.

Here was a formula for success, young exciting players picked up from schoolboy football and groomed by experienced coaches until they were ready for top flight action.

Busby played his hand just after United had won the League Championship in 1952 when seven teenagers formed the backbone of the side which went on to take the title again in 1955 and 1957.

Their names still conjure a smile to those who remember them; Duncan Edwards, Eddie Colman, Roger Byrne ... and Bobby Charlton who, unlike the majority of the famous babes, survived the Munich air disaster.

"You have to produce your own young players to succeed in this game. It may not always be possible to buy glory," says Sir Matt now in his 81st year.

And that formula is being used by Mel Machin and Jimmy Frizzell at

*Left: Paul Lake is just one of handful of promising Maine Road youngsters.*

*United's Lee Sharpe has been capped at England Under-21 level. Below: City starlet Steve Redmond.*

Maine Road as well as by present United boss Alex Ferguson.

City began their teenage revolution three seasons ago and the side which won promotion in May included young players who had led the Blues to glory in the FA Youth Cup.

Steve Redmond, Paul Lake, Andy Hinchliffe, Ian Brightwell, David White, Paul Moulden and Ian Scott have since been joined by a new generation of young ones.

Jason Beckford, Gerald Taggart, Neil Lennon and Michael Hughes have emerged bringing fresh excitement to Maine Road where Hughes is being acclaimed as another George Best.

So City are looking forward to the future but their success has not gone unnoticed at neighbouring Old Trafford where Alex Ferguson has staged a minor sensation behind the scenes by revolutionising United's scouting set-up and launching schools of excellence in three different parts of the country.

These, it is hoped, will produce the sort of young players United want and as their yardstick they can use those famous names – Bobby Charlton, George Best, Sammy McIlroy, Norman Whiteside and Mark Hughes all who have come through the Old Trafford system.

Last season Fergie plunged Russell Beardsmore, Tony Gill, Lee Martin, Lee Sharpe, Mark Robins, Deiniol Graham, David Wilson and Guiliano Maiorana into the melting pot and before the curtain finally came down Derek Brazil was the ninth United youngster to taste the big time.

Sharpe and Maiorana were the first of the exciting new finds from the United system.

So the battle is on. City versus United in the fight for teenage talent. While the hunt for the young ones goes on it can mean nothing but success for Manchester.

# WITH ALLY McCOIST

**Full name:** Alistair Murdoch McCoist.
**Date of birth:** September 24, 1962.
**Star sign:** Libra.
**Clubs:** St Johnstone, Sunderland, Rangers.

**SHOOT: Being such a busy fella off the field do you have time for any hobbies?**
ALLY: I don't have too much spare time I must admit but when I can I like to relax by listening to music – anything from Bruce Springsteen to Deacon Blue. I'm quite good friends with Marti Pellow from Wet Wet Wet and Jim Kerr from Simple Minds so I do listen to those bands too. I've even been known to wail a few bars myself from time to time – not very well I hasten to add.

**SHOOT: A lot of pro-footballers are keen golfers, would you put yourself in that category?**
ALLY: I tried to get as many rounds in as possible during the summer, but it was all to no avail. I'm still as bad as before... probably worse. I'm certainly not as good as Jimmy Nicholl or Ray 'The Bandit' Wilkins. I'm probably better when it comes to squash or snooker.

**On the footballing side, were you pleased with the way the 1988/89 season went?**
From the team's point of view, although we lost the Scottish Cup Final to Celtic, it was a great success because we recaptured the League title from our great Glasgow rivals and we lifted the Skol Cup. From a personal point of view, however, my feelings are very mixed. I had a lot of trouble with injuries after the Skol Cup win but managed to get back into my stride in time to help us win the title. The season ended on a sour note though because we lost 1-0 to Celtic at Hampden and I was disappointed with my performance. I missed a couple of chances and took some stick as a result but, as the song goes, two out of three ain't bad.

**When did your injury problems start?**
Soon after the Skol Cup Final victory over Aberdeen last October. In fact, thinking about it, I had quite a week. I scored two goals, including a late winner, in the final on the Sunday; was

sent off for a high tackle against Cologne on the Wednesday (the bloke I kicked conned the ref, though!) and then I did my hamstring against St Mirren the following Saturday. Talk about the ups and downs of football.

**Were you disappointed with your goal tally last season?**
Having scored 31, 33 and 27 League goals in the last three seasons it was difficult to come to terms with the fact that I only just made double figures in the Premier last term. It was disappointing but the thing to remember is that I missed almost half the season with injury. The only consolations were coming back in time to help the lads win the title and regaining my place in the Scotland team. I just hope my injury problems are behind me now.

**Did you manage to remain your usual cheerful self during your lay-off?**
Most of the time. There wasn't much point in moping around the place just because of an injury. We all get them from time to time. In any case if I had let the lads see me with a long face I would have got merciless stick. They are a great bunch of lads and Ibrox is a fun place to be whatever your dilemma.

**Are you the joker in the pack?**
I suppose you could say that, although towards the end of last season most of the jokes seemed to be on me. I've played pranks on most of the lads in my time – especially Davie Cooper – but they've started to backfire on me. Only recently he caught me with the old deep heat in the underpants trick. I'm always taking the mickey out of the English lads in the squad but it's all good, harmless fun. It has to be because there are so many of them these days and they can give as much as they get.

**How many members does the Ally McCoist fan club boast these days?**

*Ray Wilkins is one of the best golfers at Ibrox.*

I wouldn't dare hazard a guess because it seems to be growing all the time which is very flattering. I'm very grateful that so many people take such an interest in me and, with help from my mate Alan Ferguson, we try to answer all the mail I receive.

**What are your ambitions now?**
Although I've had six tremendously successful years at Ibrox I still haven't won a Scottish Cup winners' medal. It would be nice to put the record straight on that score this season, but the European Cup is our main priority. And, of course, it goes without saying that we want to retain the League. Oh, and I'd like to play for Scotland in the 1990 World Cup finals in Italy. Not too much to ask for, is it?

**C**hampionship darkhorses Millwall and Norwich were on course to provide one of the shocks of the century until the final furlongs of last season's title race.

Both teams, rank outsiders from the outset, made nonsense of their pre-season odds by taking the First Division by storm for two thirds of a fascinating campaign.

Sadly, for the romantic football followers at least, they slipped gracefully out of contention as grand masters Liverpool came from behind to grind their challengers down before being pipped at the post by long-time

# LIONS ROAR OUT A WARNIN

leaders Arsenal in that memorable final game of the season at Anfield.

But the efforts of the so-called no-hopers will not be forgotten in a hurry – not least by the management and players of both clubs.

## Sensation

Millwall, promoted from the Second Division only months before, caused one of the biggest sensations of the season when they topped the table early on.

According to their England prospect Alan McLeary, however, the surprise on the faces of everyone from Newquay to Newcastle did not extend to the Den.

"The fact we started so well came as no shock at all to us," reveals the

*Tony Cascarino grabbed most of The Lions' headlines.*

blond defender. "We always felt we were capable of holding our own in the top flight.

"In fact we set out with the ambition of winning the title and it was a little disappointing that we slipped out of contention around Easter.

"But we have every right to be proud of what we achieved last season. No-one will take us lightly again in the future, that's for sure."

Goal heroes Teddy Sheringham and Tony Cascarino, somewhat predictably, received most of the acclaim as the Lions roared their intentions. But the tributes shouldn't end there.

## Outstanding

"Everyone did their bit along the way," insists McLeary. "In midfield, for example, Les Briley and Terry Hurlock were outstanding.

"The defence also played their part although I believe I could have been more consistent."

That's something he intends to put right this season when he predicts that Millwall will again be in the hunt for honours.

"After last season we have no reason to fear anyone, not even Liverpool.

"If we can learn from, and build on, our experiences there's absolutely no reason at all why we can't challenge for the title and other major honours," he says.

"Nobody likes coming to the Den so there's always a chance we will get a favourable result at home and if we can get our act together away from home there's no telling what might happen."

You have been warned.

*Alan McLeary wasn't surprised at the impact Millwall made in the First Division.*

G

Rangers 'keeper Chris Woods saves from Celtic striker Mark McGhee during last season's Scottish Cup Final. A Joe Miller goal gave Celtic victory and denied Graeme Souness' men the treble.

WINNERS DON'T SMOKE BE ALL YOU CAN BE RUN SMOKE